D0186808

Aberdeenshire Library and Information Service
www.aberdeenshire.gov.uk/alis
Renewals Hotline 01224 661511

- 6 JAN 2011

26 JAN 2011

1 6 APR 2011

HEADQUARTERS

17 OCT 2011

1 0 JAN 2013

09. AUG 13. 39

02. AUG 13. 39

19/8/13 7

1 6 SEP 2013

HEADQUARTERS

1 6 JAN 2015

HEADQUARTERS

0 7 SEP 2015

0 2 SEP 2016

HEADQUARTERS

2 4 AUG 2016

COOPER, Julia

Textured knits

A L I S

1604608

TEXTURED KNITS

Quick and easy step-by-step projects

Julia Cooper

THE GUILD OF MASTER CRAFTSMAN PUBLICATIONS

A QUARTO BOOK

First published in the UK in 2004
by Guild of Master Craftsmen
166 High Street
Lewes
East Sussex B7 1XV

Copyright © 2004 Quarto Inc.

All rights reserved. No part of this
publication may be reproduced, stored in
a retrieval system, or transmitted in any
form or by any means, electronic,
mechanical, photocopying, recording or
otherwise, without the prior permission
of the copyright holder.

ISBN 1-86108-435-8

QUAR.TKN
Conceived, designed, and produced by
Quarto Publishing plc
The Old Brewery
6 Blundell Street
London N7 9BH

Knitwear designer Amanda Griffiths
Project editor Jo Fisher
Art editor Anna Knight
Designer Michelle Cannatella
Illustrator Kuo Kang Chen
Photographer Jeff Cottenden
Knitters Sandra Brown, Gill Everett
  and her team
Pattern checker Eva Yates
Text editor Margot Richardson
Proofreader Louise Armstrong
Indexer Diana LeCore
Assistant art director Penny Cobb

Art director Moira Clinch
Publisher Piers Spence

Manufactured by Universal Graphics,
Singapore
Printed by Star Standard Industries,
Singapore

9 8 7 6 5 4 3 2 1

ABERDEENSHIRE LIBRARY AND INFORMATION SERVICE	
1604608	
CAW	296736
746.432	£12.95
AD	ROSP

Contents

Introduction

Over the last few seasons a revival of interest in both the handcrafted and individual style has led to a renewed interest in the art of hand-knitting. Fashion designers have discovered once more the versatility and appeal of hand-knits, and the potential of knitting to create statements about silhouette, fabric quality and texture.

The renaissance of this craft has led to many people discovering hand-knitting to be a therapeutic and rewarding pastime: a relaxing way to use their spare time while also creating unique fashion garments. Whether you are an ardent knitting enthusiast or a complete novice with a keen interest to learn more, *Textured Knits* aims to provide a source of inspiration and a guide to textured knitting.

This book introduces the techniques and ideas that will achieve textural interest in the simplest and most effective ways, and can act as a reference for both new and more experienced knitters. The basic

skills section uses a step-by-step format to guide you, explaining the essential and basic techniques required, and introducing you to the principles of creating textured knits. It explains the possibilities that yarn provides in creating texture and demonstrates how, when used in combination with appropriate techniques, it can create particular textural effects.

The book is organized with an explanation of all the skills you will require at the beginning of the book to enable you to complete the collection of knitting projects later on. Seventeen inspirational projects have been devised by reworking traditional techniques in combination with interesting yarns to

create four distinct moods and textural statements. Among the projects is a section with cosy, comfortable, easy patterns—ideal starter projects. Another section comprises modern, contemporary patterns using clean, smooth yarns to enhance stitch structures. There is a collection of cable sweaters and rugged knits using tweed and rustic yarns. And finally a collection of antique-inspired knits using lace-work and beading techniques.

Textured knits are easily achievable and will indulge you in the experience of working with wonderfully tactile yarn. Discover the satisfaction of creating your own unique garment or article as you while away the stresses of modern life, giving yourself the perfect excuse to relax!

BASIC SKILLS

This section introduces you to all the basic knitting skills you need to get started. It is structured in a step-by-step format that teaches you how to hold the needles, cast on stitches and master various stitch combinations. This will enable you to work through the projects and create a variety of surface qualities and textured knits.

Essentials

All you need to create a knitted fabric is a ball of yarn and a pair of knitting needles. However, as your skills and ambitions progress, you will find that to achieve successful results, it is important to acquire the right materials and equipment. Your range of accessories will grow along with your experience.

Knitting needles

A pair of knitting needles is the most essential piece of equipment. Needles are available in a number of sizes to suit the type of yarn you are using. When selecting a pair of needles, ensure that:

- they are the correct size for the yarn
- they are long enough to hold the width of the fabric being knitted (needles can come in different lengths)
- they are strong enough to hold the yarn
- they are smooth so that the yarn won't snag.

Needles are also available in a variety of materials: bamboo, aluminium or plastic. Which material you select is down to personal preference or availability.

Knitting needles come in three main forms. The most commonly used are:

- two simple smooth sticks with an end to stop the knitting stitches falling off
- circular needles: two short needles joined together by a nylon or thin metal cord, which allow you to work in the round to create a seamless fabric
- double-pointed needles: come in sets of four or five and allow you to work in the round and change direction easily.

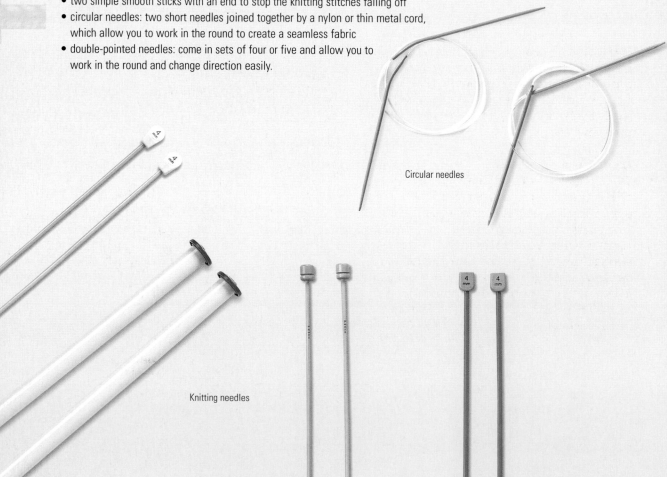

Circular needles

Knitting needles

Needle sizes

Needles come in different diameters so that the knitted stitch achieves the correct tension (see page 17) for the article being made. There is no universal guide for knitting needle sizes and they fall into three main categories:

- American: the needle sizes are given numbers, and range from 0 to 15, with the diameter increasing as the number gets larger
- Metric: these are the most commonly used in Europe. They give the actual diameter of the needle in millimetres. Sizes start at 2 mm and go up to 20 mm
- Imperial (also known as British): an old UK sizing which is still used by some knitters and ranges from 14 to 000. It works in the opposite way to the American system in that the higher the number, the smaller the needle size.

Needle size conversion chart

US	Metric (mm)	Old UK/ Canadian
36	20	–
19	15	–
17	12	–
15	10	000
13	9	00
11	8	0
10½	7½	1
10½	7	2
10½	6½	3
10	6	4
9	5½	5
8	5	6
7	4½	7
6	4	8

Needle gauge

A needle gauge has a series of holes running down the centre. Push the needle through the holes until you find the correct diameter. This can be especially useful if using old needles bought from a charity shop as size is not marked on all needles.

Cable needles

Cable needles are used to hold stitches while you cross or transfer stitches from one needle to another for cable or Aran patterns. They are available in the same sizes as standard knitting needles and, providing you are not using a needle size that is too large for the stitch size, you don't have to have exactly the same size as your main knitting needle. Cable needles can be double-ended and straight, or shaped in the middle to prevent the chance of stitches slipping off the needle. Both do the same job and whichever you use is a matter of preference.

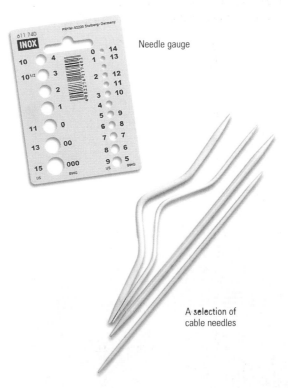

Needle gauge

A selection of cable needles

Stitch markers

Stitch markers are usually brightly coloured, circular and look like a small coil with a split on one side. Stitch markers are used to mark stitch detailing, such as increases and decreases and cable positions. They are also a useful way of marking the beginning of new rows when you are using circular needles or sets of four needles.

Stitch holders

A stitch holder looks like a large safety pin and is used to hold stitches before casting off or adding a detail, such as a neckline, to the work. You can use safety pins instead, but they tend to be sharp and may split the yarn.

Stitch holders

Stitch markers

Row counter

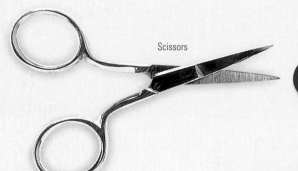

Scissors

Tape-measure

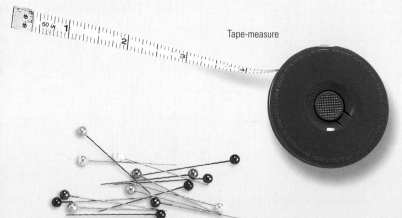

Row counters

A row counter is a small cylinder with a hole running through the centre and rotating numbers inside it. You have to remember to turn the dial at the end of every row, since the row counter does not count automatically.

Scissors and tape-measure

Small, sharp scissors and a good tape-measure are essential. The best tape-measures for knitters are the retractable dressmaking type. It is best to have one marked with both inches and centimetres.

Pins

The best pins to use on knitted fabric are long with brightly coloured tips.

Pins

Sewing needles

Knitters' sewing needles are large and blunt. They have different-sized eyes to accommodate various plies of yarn. For sewing chunkier knits, you need a ball-ended needle or bodkin.

Sewing needles

Point protectors

Point protectors are made from flexible plastic or rubber, and are like a small tag with two holes for the needle to slip into. As the name suggests, point protectors are used to keep the needle points from becoming damaged, to eliminate the risk of work sliding off the needles and to protect the knitter from an accidental jab while the piece is in a workbag.

Point protector

Pom-pom maker

You can make pom-poms by winding yarn around pieces of cardboard, but plastic pom-pom makers last well and have a groove around them that makes it easier to cut through the yarn.

Graph paper

Mohair brush

A mohair brush generally has small metal teeth. It is used to brush fabric made from mohair to create a furry texture.

Graph paper

Graph paper is essential when designing your own patterns for plotting motifs or pattern details.

Pom-pom maker

Bags and baskets

Essential for storing work and equipment.

Mohair brush

Storage basket

Yarns

Selecting yarn is one of the most important decisions you will have to make as a knitter as it will strongly influence the look of your article. There are various characteristics to consider: the thickness or ply of the yarn, the fibre content, and the manufacturer's treatment of the fibre. Thick yarns tend to produce bulkier fabrics and thinner yarns produce finer ones. Fibres can be from animal, plant or synthetic origin, and each fibre has specific properties that will affect the knitted fabric. In addition, the fibre can be treated and spun to make it heavier, denser, twisted, flatter, knobblier, lighter or hairier. It is the combination of these factors that creates the tactile qualities of yarn, which in turn will determine the texture and character of your knitted article.

Yarns from animals

Wool

Wool is the most common yarn used in knitting and is a great warm, winter yarn. It is a very durable and easy yarn to work with, and is good for plain knitting. Its natural elasticity means it is good for rib and cable fabrics that need to pull in and stretch. It is a very versatile fibre and blends well with other yarns. It can be either fine and delicate, or heavier and more rugged depending on how it is spun. It is often spun with a smooth appearance which makes it ideal for showing stitch detail.

Mohair

Mohair is often classed as a fashion yarn due to its unique hairy fabric surface. Some people dislike it; they feel it is too fluffy and irritating, but it is now often blended with other fibres to overcome this. The types used in this book are mixed with wool and with silk to give a fine, discreet appearance and a refined, luxury feel.

Silk

Silk is available in two qualities: wild, which produces a coarse thread, and cultivated, which produces a finer thread. Both are expensive and so silk is often associated with luxury. As a knitting yarn on its own it can be brittle, so its non-elastic quality means it is not suitable for clinging or stretchy stitches. For this reason it is often blended with other fibres to make it more versatile.

Angora and cashmere

Both these fibres are expensive but have a wonderfully soft and luxurious feel. Cashmere can be used in its pure form but, due to its expense, is much more widely used blended with another fibre such as silk or wool. Angora is more commonly used blended with wool and often sheds the hairs from the rabbit fur.

Yarns from plants

Cotton

Cotton is made from a natural plant fibre and, although historically used as a summer yarn, is warm in the winter and cool in the summer. It generally has a smooth appearance, and can be crisp or soft depending on how it has been produced. It is good for showing stitch detail and, depending on how it has been finished, can have a matt or mercerised, glazed effect.

Linen

Linen is made from the stem of a flax plant. It is very strong and washes well. It absorbs moisture so is often good in hot climates. Linen can be stiff and has a tendency to crease so it is often blended with other fibres such as cotton to make it easier to wear and work with.

Synthetic or man-made yarns

Nylon, polyester, acrylic and rayon

Synthetic yarn fibres are easy and inexpensive to produce and can be useful alternatives for allergy sufferers. However, they can be rather warm to wear and cheap in appearance. Nylon, acrylic and polyester are most commonly used blended with other plant or animal fibres to give stability to delicate or fragile fibres or yarn mixes.

Yarn types used in this book

Jaeger Extra Fine Merino Double Knitting

Jaeger Matchmaker Merino Aran

Rowan Magpie Aran

Rowanspun Double Knitting

Rowan Polar

Rowan Kid Classic

Rowan Kid Silk Haze

Jaeger Aqua Cotton Double Knitting

Rowan All Seasons Cotton

Rowan Wool Cotton Double Knitting

Rowan Chunky Cotton Chenille

Rowan Cotton Glace

Jaeger Extra Fine Merino Double Knitting 100% wool
Jaeger Matchmaker Merino Aran 100% wool
Rowan Magpie Aran 100% wool
Rowanspun Double Knitting 100% wool
Rowan Polar 60% wool, 30% alpaca, 10% acrylic
Rowan Kid Classic 70% lambswool, 26% kid mohair, 4% nylon

Rowan Kid Silk Haze 70% superkid mohair, 30% silk
Jaeger Aqua Cotton Double Knitting 100% cotton
Rowan All Seasons Cotton (Aran weight) 60% cotton, 40% acrylic
Rowan Wool Cotton Double Knitting 50% wool, 50% cotton
Rowan Chunky Cotton Chenille 100% cotton
Rowan Cotton Glace 100% cotton

TEXTURED KNITS

Buying and substituting yarn

In general it is best to buy the specific yarn that is suggested in the pattern (see page 128 for a list of suppliers). However, in some cases, if the yarn specified is not available, you may have to substitute a yarn, or you may prefer another yarn.

A number of factors are important when selecting another yarn. The ply, or thickness, must be similar so that you can achieve the correct tension in the pattern. You should check that the yarn property will give you the effect that you want. Check the yardage so that you know how much yarn to buy; the weight can vary between each yarn type, so the length of yarn needed is a more accurate guide. It is always a good idea to buy an extra ball anyway, in case of mistakes.

Reading the ball band

When choosing your yarn, remember to check the information on the ball band. You should knit your garment with yarn from the same dye lot because different dye lots can vary in tone.

Gauge guide

Needle size

Yarn content

Shade and dye lot

Yardage

Yarn weight

Care instructions

Rowan Yarns
Holmfirth
England

SEE OVER FOR
ALTERNATIVE
CARE INSTRUCTIONS

22-24 sts
10 cm/4 in
30-32 rows
10 cm/4 in

9-8
UK
5-6
US
3¾-4
mm

R O W A N

wool cotton

50% MERINO WOOL 50% COTTON
50% MERINO WOLLE 50% BAUMWOLLE
50% MERINO LAINE 50% COTTON

SH953   LOT5C2

5 013712 920028

In accordance with B S 984
Approx Length 113m (123 yds)

50g

www.rowanyarns.co.uk

Warm (40° C) Wool Cycle, minimum machine action

Cool iron

Do not bleach

Dry clean in certain solvents

Do not tumble dry Dry flat out of direct sunlight

Importance of Tension

It is very important to achieve the correct tension when knitting. It is the key to knitting the correct size and achieving the fabric quality intended for the article. All the knitting patterns in this book include a recommended tension to work to. If you do not match the tension, your work may not fit correctly.

Measuring tension

Knit a swatch with the size of needles given in the pattern instructions and using the yarn you have selected for your project. Add a few extra stitches and work a few more rows than specified in the tension check, as the edge stitches can be distorted. Gently press your swatch, after checking the yarn-care instructions on the ball band so as not to damage your fabric. Place your tension swatch on a flat surface.

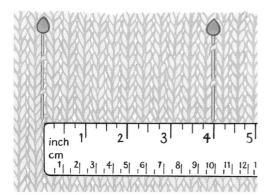

1 Count and mark the stitches with pins, then measure between the pins. If the measurement is correct, you'll know that your finished garment will be the right width. If your marked stitches measure less, you're knitting too tightly and the garment will be too narrow. Knit another swatch using slightly larger needles, and measure again. If the marked stitches measure more than they should, you're knitting too loosely and the garment will be too wide. Knit another swatch on slightly smaller needles, and measure again.

2 Mark the number of rows and check the measurement. If it's correct, go ahead and start knitting. If the marked rows measure less, your knitting is tight, and the garment will be too short. Try using slightly larger needles for your next swatch. If the marked rows measure more than they should, your knitting is loose and the garment will be too long. Try knitting another swatch using slightly smaller needles.

Too tight

Correct gauge

Too loose

Reading Patterns

Once you have selected the item you want to make, it is important that you read through the whole pattern before you start to knit.

Most of the patterns in this book have multiple sizes, except for a few projects that are one size only. The smallest sizes are given first with subsequent ones in brackets. There are usually at least three finished measurements included to help you select the correct size: the chest/bust measurement, taken under the arm across the chest; the length, which is taken from the back neck to the very bottom edge of the garment; and finally the sleeve length, which is taken from the cuff to the underarm point.

Recommended yarn type and quantity appear at the beginning of the pattern along with any additional items you may require such as zips, buttons or beads.

The suggested needle size is always stated in order to achieve the recommended tension. Any additional needles, such as cable needles, or specific knitting accessories are also listed.

Most knitting patterns use at least some abbreviations or knitting terminology. Many of these are explained in the skills section in this book and are fairly logical and easy to understand. The following list of general terms and abbreviations are used throughout the book. Any special abbreviations for particular projects are listed at the beginning of each pattern.

Abbreviations

ABCD etc	Contrasting colours as indicated in colour key of patterns
approx	approximately
cm	centimetre(s)
dec	decrease
g	grams
in	inch(es)
inc	increase
k	knit
k2tog	knit two stitches together
LH	left-hand
m	metre(s)
mb	move bead
MB	make bobble
ML	make loop
mm	millimetre(s)
oz	ounce(s)
p	purl
patt	pattern
psso	pass slipped stitch over
RH	right-hand
RS	right side
sl 1	slip one stitch
st(s)	stitch(es)
tog	together
WS	wrong side
yd	yard(s)
yf	yarn forward
yo	yarn over
( )	repeat instructions inside these brackets until
*	asterisks are used to show a set of instructions that need to be repeated

124 Antique Knits

PROJECT 17:
Lace Cardigan

This cardigan uses a faggotted rib pattern to create the illusion of a combination of lace, rib and slip stitch textures. The decadent feel is enhanced by a glazed yarn and beaded buttons.

Materials
Yarn: 10 (10, 11) x 50 g balls Jaeger Aqua 100% cotton DK, Shade 306/DK cotton, grey (approx 106 m (115 yd) per 50 g (1¾ oz ball))
Needles: 4 mm (size 6) and 3.75 mm (size 5)
Other: 10 buttons

Check your gauge
22 sts x 30 rows to 10 x 10 cm (4 x 4 in) measured over stockinette stitch using 4 mm (size 6) needles.

Abbreviations
See page 16.

Left front
Cast on 50 (55, 60) sts using 3.75 mm (size 5) needles.
Change to 4 mm (size 6) needles.
Work in pattern throughout as follows:
Row 1: (RS) k1 , * k2tog, yf, k1, yf, k1, psso, rep from * to last 9 sts, k1, k5, yf, k2tog, k1.
Row 2: (WS) Purl.
Rows 1-2 form pattern repeat.
Rows 3-90: Work in pattern.

Shape armhole
Row 91: (RS) Bind off 3 sts, work to end.
Row 92: (WS) Purl to end.
Row 93: (RS) Bind off 1 st, work to end.
Row 94: Purl to end.
Rows 95-102: Repeat rows 93-94 four times until 42 (47, 52) sts on needle.
Rows 103-121: Work without shaping.

Shape neck
Row 122: (WS) Bind off 10 sts, purl to end.
Row 123: (RS) Pattern to end.
Row 124: Bind off 2 sts, to end.
Row 125: Pattern to end.
Row 126: Bind off 1 st, purl to end.
Rows 127-136: Repeat rows 125-126 five times until 24 (29, 34) sts on needle.
Rows 137-140: Work in pattern without shaping.

Shape shoulder
Row 141: (RS) Bind off 8 sts, pattern to end.
Row 142: Purl to end.
Rows 149-150: Repeat rows 141-148 6 (13, 18) sts on needle)
Row 151: Bind off.

Sizes	Small	Medium	Large
To fit bust cm (in)	86 (34)	91 (36)	97 (38)
Actual size	91 (36)	97 (38)	102 (40)
Back length	55 (22)	55 (22)	55 (22)
Sleeve underarm	47 (18½)	47 (18½)	47 (18½)

Reading charts

A chart is occasionally included in some pattern instructions in addition to the normal directions. Charts are used for specific stitch work or patterning that is easier to convey visually rather than through written instruction. A key is included to explain all symbols.

Each small square on a chart represents one stitch and the chart should be read from the bottom right-hand corner. The first row and all odd-numbered rows are usually right side rows and should be read from right to left. Even-numbered rows (wrong side) should be read from left to right.

Key to charts:

☐ k on RS, p on WS

▨ p on RS, k on WS

Hold 3 sts on cable needle at front of work, k next 3 sts, then k3 sts from cable needle

Hold 3 sts on cable needle at back of work, k next 3 sts, then k3 sts from cable needle

A series of symbols is used to denote stitches, specific knitting instructions or colours

If a pattern repeat is formed, this is marked on the chart and should be repeated until otherwise instructed in the written pattern

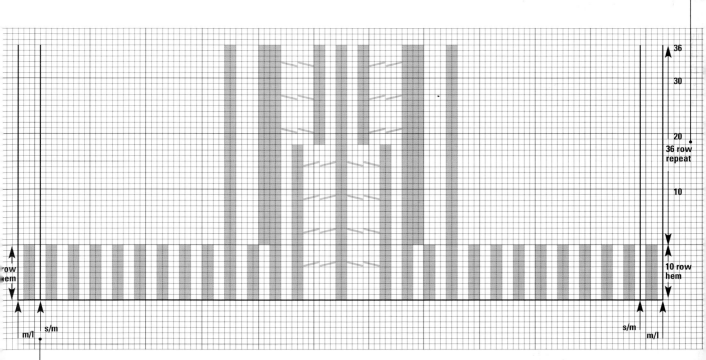

Different sizes are marked so the chart can be adjusted to whichever size you require

Holding the Needles

There are a variety of ways to hold the needles. The one you adopt depends on what feels most comfortable to you and achieves the most successful results. Whether you are right- or left-handed, one of the three following techniques should suit you.

Scottish or English method

Both needles are held from above. The left hand holds both the needles leaving the right hand to make the stitch. Wrap the yarn around the fingers of your right hand, taking the yarn around the little finger, over the ring finger, under the middle finger, and over the forefinger. Hold the yarn at the back for a knit stitch and at the front for a purl stitch. Use your left hand to move the stitches up the left needle, and your right hand to guide the right needle in and out of the stitches.

French method

This is very similar to the Scottish method. The only difference is the way the right needle is held. Hold the yarn as in the Scottish method, but hold the right needle underneath as if it were a pencil. Use your forefinger on your right hand to guide the yarn.

German or Continental method

Here, the yarn is held in the left hand. Hold both the needles as in the Scottish method. Wrap the yarn over your left little finger and over the top of your forefinger. Use the right needle to make the stitch, controlling the yarn with your left hand.

Casting On

The key to casting on is an even tension that allows you to work the first knitting row easily.
There are various ways to achieve a good cast-on edge.

Making a slip knot

Most cast-on methods rely on making an initial stitch which enables other stitches
to be made. This first stitch is best made using a slip knot.

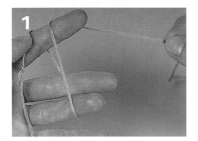
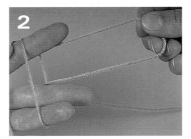
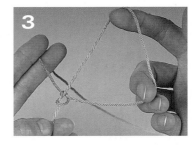

1 Make a loop in the yarn by wrapping it around the three middle fingers of your left hand in a clockwise directon.

2 Pass the yarn held in your right hand under the existing loop to form a second loop.

3 Place this loop on the needle, remove your fingers from the left-hand loop, and pull the yarn to tighten.

Thumb method cast-on

To cast on using this method, you need two lengths of yarn that are worked simultaneously.
The slip knot that forms the first stitch must be far enough along the yarn to create two ends,
so that one is free and the other is attached to the ball.

To gauge how long this tail end of yarn needs to be, you will need to do a simple calculation.
For example, if your finished cast-on edge (i.e. width of garment) is 40 cm (16 in), you will
need a 120 cm (48 in) length of yarn, three times the width of the finished knitted piece.

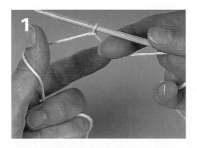
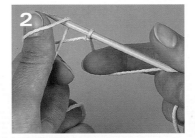
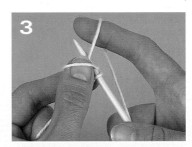

1 Place the slip knot on the needle and hold the needle in your right hand. *Take the tail end of yarn around your left thumb in a clockwise direction to form a loop.

2 Slide the needle upward through the loop on your thumb

3 Take the yarn held in your right hand counter-clockwise around the needle from back to front.

4 Transfer the loop from your thumb on to the needle and pull the end to tighten. Repeat from *.

TEXTURED KNITS

Long tail cast-on

This method is also known as the German, or double cable method.

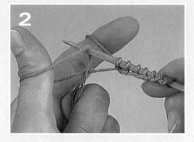

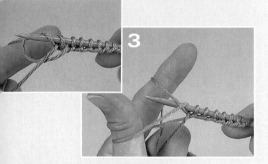

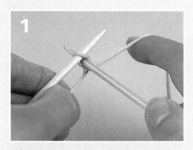

1 Place the slip knot on the needle, leaving a long tail, and hold the needle in your right hand. *Wrap the free end of yarn around your left thumb from front to back. Place the other yarn over your left forefinger and hold both threads in the palm of your hand.

2 Slide the needle up through the loop on your thumb and over the top of the yarn on your forefinger.

3 Draw the yarn through the loop on your thumb. Transfer the loop from your thumb to the needle and pull to tighten. Repeat from *.

Cable method cast-on

This method uses both needles and gives a strong cast-on edge.

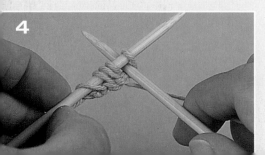

1 Place the slip knot on the left-hand needle. Slide the right needle upward through the knot from front to back. Take the yarn in your right hand around the right needle in a clockwise direction from back to front.

2 Slide the needle down and back through the knot, catching the wrapped yarn and making a loop on the right needle.

3 Place the left needle under and up through the front of the loop on the right needle. Remove the right needle, thus transferring the stitch on to the left needle.

4 To make subsequent stitches, work the same process, but begin by placing the right needle between the first two stitches on the left needle.

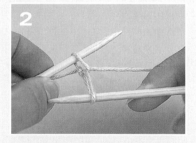

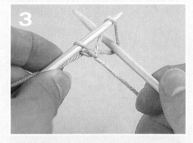

Invisible cast-on

This method can only be worked on a single rib. Using a contrasting coloured yarn, cast on half the number of stitches required, using the cable method. An even number of stitches is needed, so cast on one extra if need be.

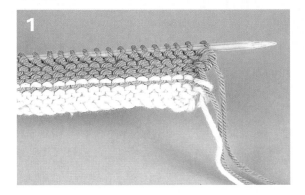

1 Work a row of purl, then a row of knit in the first yarn, then work four subsequent rows of stocking stitch in the yarn required to complete the knitted piece.

2 On the next row, purl one stitch from the left needle. Using the right needle, pick up a loop in the same colour from the row where the contrasting yarn finished.

3 *Place the loop on the left-hand needle. Take the yarn to the back of the work and knit the stitch.

4 Purl the next stitch on the left needle, then pick up the next loop along from the row where the colour changed and repeat from *.

5 When the row is completed, unravel the contrast yarn.

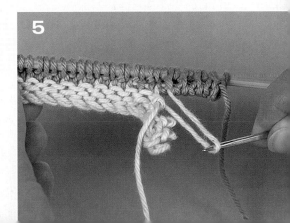

Knit and Purl

There are two basic knitting stitches—knit and purl. These stitches form the basis of all knitted fabrics so once you have mastered them you will have the opportunity to create even the most complicated knitted textures.

Basic method

Making a knit stitch

1 *Holding the yarn at the back, insert the right needle upward through the first stitch on the left needle from front to back.

2 Take the yarn around the needle in a counter-clockwise direction from back to front.

3 Using the tip of the right needle, draw a loop of yarn through the stitch on the left needle to form a loop on the right needle. Then slip the original stitch off the left needle. Repeat these three steps from *.

Making a purl stitch

 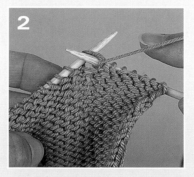 

1 *Holding the yarn at the front of the work, insert the right needle downward through the first stitch on the left needle from right to left.

2 Take the yarn around the needle in a counter-clockwise direction, and back to the front.

3 Lower the tip of the right needle, taking it away from you, to draw a loop of yarn through the stitch on the left needle to form a loop on the right needle. Then slip the original stitch off the left needle. Repeat these three steps from *.

German or Continental method

If you use this method, the yarn is held in your left hand and therefore knit and purl stitches are worked in a different way.

Making a knit stitch

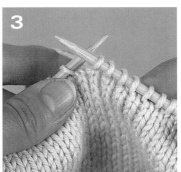

1 Hold the yarn at the back of the work and over your left index finger.

2 Insert the right needle up through the first stitch from front to back. Take the right needle around behind the yarn on your left finger from right to left.

3 Using the right needle, draw the yarn through the centre of the stitch on the left needle.

4 Slip the original stitch from the left needle, leaving the new stitch on the right needle.

Making a purl stitch

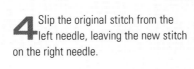

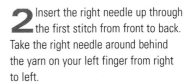

1 Hold the yarn at the front of the work under your left thumb.

2 Insert the right needle through the first stitch on the left needle from right to left, over the yarn held by your thumb, thus making a loop around the needle.

3 Using the right needle, push the looped yarn backward through the original stitch.

4 Slip the original stitch from the left needle, leaving the new stitch on the right needle.

Turning the work

At the end of every row, whether it is a knit or a purl row, you will need to turn the work in order to start the next row. The left needle becomes the empty one, as the stitches are transferred to the right needle as you progress along the row. Once all the stitches are on the right needle, simply transfer the left needle to the right hand, and the right needle to the left hand, and begin to work the next row.

In some instances, such as when shaping a neck, or working the heel of a sock, you may be instructed to turn the work part-way through a row. In which case simply turn the work around so that the opposite side is facing you and begin to work again as instructed.

How to slip a stitch knitwise or purlwise

In some instances, it is necessary to pass a stitch from one needle to another needle. This is known as slipping a stitch. The way this stitch is slipped can determine how it sits on the needle, so a pattern may instruct you to slip the stitch either knitwise or purlwise.

To slip a stitch knitwise insert the right needle into the stitch as if to knit it, but then just slip it from the left needle to the right needle.

To slip purlwise insert the right needle into the stitch as if to purl it, but then just slip it from the left needle to the right needle.

Casting Off

Once you have completed your knitted piece it needs to be secured so that it does not unravel. There are a number of ways this can be done, but to complete the projects in this book you will need to master only the knit and purl cast-off techniques.

Basic knit cast-off

This is the most commonly used casting off technique, and, unless otherwise instructed in the pattern, it should be assumed that this is the cast-off method to use.

1 Knit the first two stitches from the left needle, so that two new stitches sit on the right needle. *Holding the yarn at the back, insert the left needle through the base of the first stitch on the right needle from left to right.

2 Bring the first stitch over the top of the second stitch, and slip it off the right needle.

3 One stitch is now remaining on the right needle, knit the next stitch from the left needle and repeat from *.

Basic purl cast-off

1 Purl the first two stitches from the left needle, so that two new stitches sit on the right needle. *Holding the yarn at the back, insert the left needle through the base of the first stitch on the right needle from left to right.

2 Bring the first stitch over the top of the second stitch, and slip it off the right needle.

3 One stitch is now remaining on the right needle, purl the next stitch from the left needle and repeat from *.

Knit and Purl Textures

Simple textured patterns can be created using a combination of the knit and purl stitch techniques. The type of pattern formed depends on the sequence the stitches take within each row, and how each of the rows is repeated.

Garter stitch

Garter stitch is created by working knit or purl stitches every row. It produces a ridged-looking fabric that appears the same on each side.

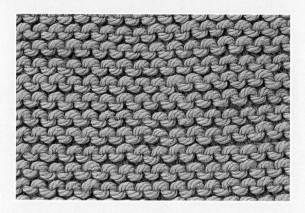

Stocking stitch

Stocking stitch is created by working a knit row, and then a purl row, in repeats. This produces a smooth-looking fabric that is quite flat in appearance on one side.

Reverse stocking stitch

This stitch is, in effect, the reverse side of stocking stitch. It is created by working a purl row, then a knit row, in repeats.

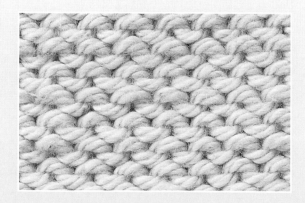

Moss stitch

Moss stitch, or seed stitch as it is also known, is created by working a combination of alternate knit and purl stitches in the same row. However, on subsequent rows the stitches are worked so that they do not match up to the row before. For example, on the next row, a purl stitch sits on top of a knit stitch, and a knit stitch on top of a purl stitch—thus creating a check-effect texture.

Rib textures

Rib stitch patterns are created by working knit and purl stitches alternately along the same row. On subsequent rows, matching knit and purl stitches line up on top of each other to form vertical ridges on both sides of the work. Ribs can be in a variety of combinations, either regular or irregular. They are often found at the beginning of a garment, as they have an elastic quality which keeps compact, creating a neat and firm edge to a piece of knitting.

2x2 This rib is created by knitting 2 stitches, then purling 2 stitches, and repeating to the end of the row. These stitches are matched on subsequent rows.

1x1 This rib is created by knitting 1 stitch, then purling the next stitch, and repeating to the end of the row. These stitches are matched on subsequent rows.

TEXTURED KNITS

Cable and Bobble Textures

Cables

Knitting groups of stitches in various sequences can create a variety of raised textures and criss-crossing stitch patterns. Traditionally associated with Fisherman's or Aran sweaters, cables can be worked over two or more stitches and can make a number of plaits, diamonds and coiling stitch patterns by moving stitches to the front or back of each other.

How to cable

Once you understand the principle of the cable technique, it is possible to create a variety of textural cable relief patterns.

In order to cable or twist a group of stitches, it is necessary to introduce a short double-ended needle to transfer the stitches. When the cable needle is held at the front of the work, the stitches make a diagonal from right to left. When the needle is held at the back of the work, the stitches make a diagonal from left to right. Depending on the repetition and sequence of these twists, any number of cables can be created.

Back cable

This four-stitch cable crosses at the back and all four stitches are knitted.

1 Slip the first two stitches on to a cable needle and hold at the back of the work, then knit the next two stitches from the left needle.

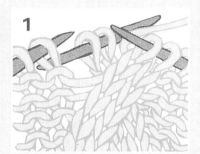

2 Knit the two stitches from the cable needle.

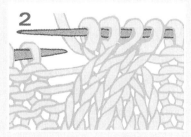

Front cable

This four-stitch cable crosses at the front and all four stitches are knitted.

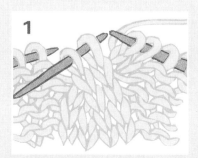

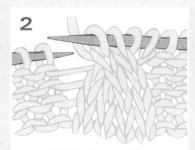

1 Slip the first two stitches on to a cable needle and hold at the front of the work, then knit the next two stitches from the left needle.

2 Knit the two stitches from the cable needle.

Front travelling cable

This four-stitch cable crosses at the front, with two knit stitches moving to the left on a reverse stocking stitch background.

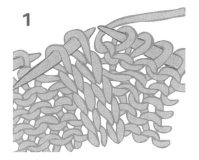

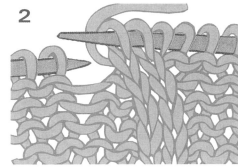

1 Slip the first two stitches on to a cable needle and hold at the front of work. Then, purl the next two stitches from the left needle..

2 Knit the two stitches from the cable needle.

Back travelling cable

This four-stitch cable crosses at the back, with two knit stitches moving to the right on a reverse stocking stitch background.

1 Slip the first two stitches on to a cable needle and hold at the back of the work, then knit the next two stitches from the left needle.

2 Purl the two stitches from the cable needle.

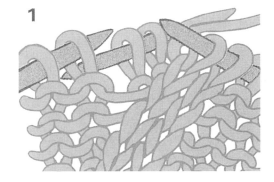

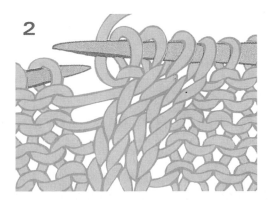

Bobbles

By using a combination of increases and decreases you can create three-dimensional textural areas in your fabric. A group of stitches that is increased and worked into, then decreased abruptly, can create a cluster of raised knots or bobbles.

Making a three-stitch bobble

Bobbles are always started on the right side of a knitted fabric.
This bobble is small and created over three stitches.

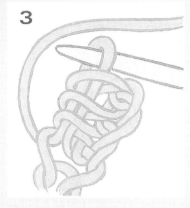

1 Work to where you want the bobble. Work into the next stitch on the left needle and create extra stitches by casting on three stitches.

2 Knit the three cast-on stitches, then knit the original stitch again, making four new stitches on the right needle.

3 To complete the bobble, lift the three stitches, one at a time, over the last stitch on the right needle.

Making a five-stitch bobble

Bobbles are always worked on the right side of the fabric. In this example, it is on a reverse stocking stitch background.

1 Work to where you want the bobble. Work into the next stitch on the left needle and create extra stitches by working into the front and back of this stitch until five stitches are on the right needle.

2 Then, turn and purl the five stitches.

3 To complete the bobble, turn, knit five stitches, turn, purl two stitches together, purl one stitch, then purl two stitches together, turn, slip two stitches knitwise, knit one, then pass the slipped stitches over the last knit stitch. Alternatively, you can decrease the five stitches by working all five stitches together at once so that only one stitch remains.

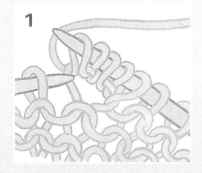

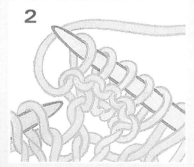

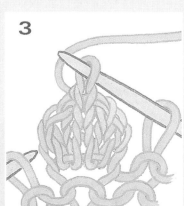

Lace Textures

Lace-stitch patterns are created by a combination of decreased and increased stitches within a row. The arrangement of these increases (which form holes) and decreases (which compensate for the extra stitches made) are worked in a way to form a textural pattern. There are a number of commonly used stitch techniques which form the basis of lace knitting.

Making an extra stitch to form a hole

In order to create lace patterns it is necessary to form holes or eyelets in the knitted fabric. The type of lace pattern created depends on where these holes are placed, and how often they occur. These holes are created by using the "yarn over" technique, which involves moving the yarn to the front or back of the work depending on which stitch you are going to work next.

The position of the yarn, whether it is at the front or back of the work, is very important in lace knitting and is often clearly stated within the pattern instructions. By moving the yarn backward or forward over the needle, you can create an extra stitch or extra multiple stitches, which when worked into on the next row can create a hole or multiple holes to form a lace pattern.

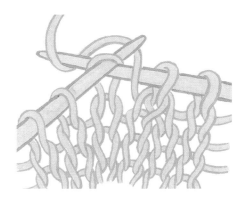

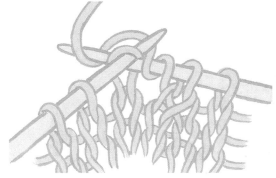

Yarn over

To make a yarn over between knit stitches, bring the yarn to the front as if to purl, knit the next stitch by inserting the right needle into the next stitch on the left needle from front to back, then take the yarn back so you can finish knitting the stitch. An extra stitch will have been formed.

Multiple yarn over

For larger holes, or a sequence of holes, more than one yarn over may be required. Bring the yarn to the front, and take it over the needle. Then bring it to the front and over the needle again for each following yarn over.

Decreasing a stitch to balance a pattern

To compensate for the extra stitches created to make holes in lace knitting, certain stitches should be decreased either within the same row or on subsequent rows. These decreases can slant to the right or left depending on the pattern-effect required.

Right-slanting decreases
By knitting two stitches together, you can balance a yarn over.

1 Insert the right needle through the front of the first two stitches on the left needle, then take the yarn around the needle.

2 Draw the loop through and drop the two stitches off the left needle.

Multiple right-slanting decreases
By knitting or purling together more than two stitches, you can balance multiple yarn overs or extra stitches. The illustration shows three stitches decreased together.

Count the number of stitches to work into on the left needle. Insert the right needle tip into the front of the third stitch, then through the fronts of the other two stitches, take the yarn around the needle in the usual way, draw the new stitch through all three stitches and drop them off the left needle together.

Left-slanting decreases
By slipping a stitch, knitting the next stitch, then lifting the slipped stitch over the stitch just knitted, you will have decreased a stitch as the first stitch is lying over the second, thus balancing yarn over.

1 Insert the right needle knitwise through the front of the first stitch on the left needle, and slip it on to the right. Knit the next stitch.

2 Use the tip of the left needle to lift the slipped stitch over the knitted stitch and off the right needle.

Multiple left-slanting decreases
To balance a multiple yarn over, you can combine the technique of slipping stitches and working stitches together to compensate for any additional stitches made in the lace pattern.

Slip the first stitch knitwise, knit the next two (or more) stitches together, then lift the first stitch over as shown. The first stitch lies on top, so the decrease slants to the left.

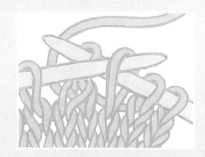

Knitting with Beads

Before beginning to knit using beads, it is necessary to thread them on to the yarn before even casting on. It will often not be possible to thread the knitting yarn directly through the bead. To thread the beads on to your yarn easily, thread a sewing needle using both ends of a sewing thread. Place the yarn through the loop of thread, then pass the beads over the eye of the needle and on to both threads and then on to the yarn itself.

You will need to estimate the quantity of beads needed for each ball of yarn. If these get used up before the ball is finished, break the yarn at the end of a row and thread a fresh quantity of beads on.

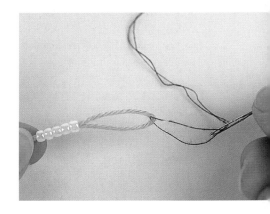

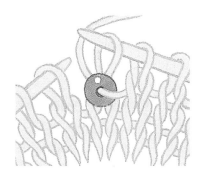

Placing a bead using a slip stitch

Placing beads using a slip-stitch technique is done by working on the right side of stocking stitch. It can be used for both small and larger beads as it does not interrupt the knitted stitch.

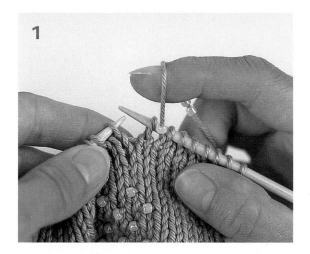

1 Work to where the bead is required. Slide the bead up the yarn. Bring the yarn forward between the needles with the bead to the front and slip the next stitch purlwise.

2 Keep the bead as close to the knitting as possible, holding it in front of the slipped stitch with a finger or thumb if necessary, then take the yarn back between the needles leaving the yarn in front. Knit the next stitch firmly.

Additional Textures

By using many of the techniques previously covered, you will find it is possible to create a number of additional textural stitches. By using the yarn over technique demonstrated in the lace section (pages 33 and 34), you will be able to create elongated stitches. In addition, by using the principles of working into the front and back of a stitch to increase and make multiple stitches, you will be able to create loops on the surface of your fabric for extreme textural impact.

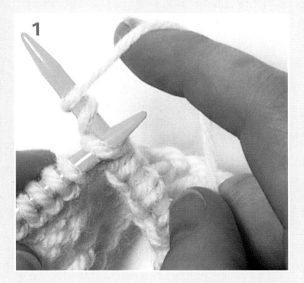

Lengthened stitch

A lengthened stitch, or dropped stitch, is formed by wrapping the yarn two or more times around the needle, rather than only once as is usually required to make the next stitch.

Instead of decreasing these extra stitches, as often done in lace work, these extra stitches are worked in a different way. On the following row, the extra stitches, or loops created by the multiple yarn overs, are dropped off in order to create a long or elongated stitch.

1 Insert the right needle knitwise in the required stitch and wrap the yarn twice around the needle tip, instead of once.

2 Pull the double loop through in the same way as when knitting a stitch.

3 On the following row, the double loop may be worked as knit or purl, according to the pattern; here the right needle is shown inserted knitwise. Work the stitch and drop the extra loop from the needle.

Loop stitch

Loops are formed on the right side of the work. Therefore, this stitch is usually worked on alternate plain knit or purl rows to allow the loops to be more evident and create more textural impact.

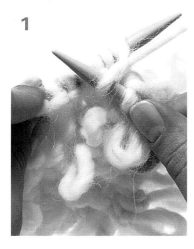

1 With the right side facing you, knit into the stitch that is to be worked as a loop, but do not let it slip off the left needle.

2 Bring the yarn forward between needles and wind once clockwise around your left thumb. Take yarn back again between the needles.

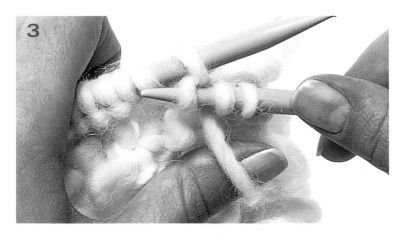

3 Knit again into the same stitch on the left-hand needle (making two stitches on the right-hand needle).

4 Withdraw your thumb from the stitch. Pass the first stitch over the loop stitch to secure it. Then, work to the next stitch in the pattern that needs to be a loop stitch.

Shaping, Joining and Making Up

In order to complete the projects in this book and work your knitted fabrics into finished articles, it will be necessary for you to learn the basic techniques of shaping, joining and making up.

To shape a knitted piece, you must understand the principles of the decreasing and increasing techniques, to enable you to make your fabrics narrower or wider. By adopting certain joining methods, you will be able to achieve a neat and professional finish, and by following and understanding the importance of simple working methods, you will find the making up process easier and achieve successful finished results.

Shaping techniques

When knitting you can shape at the same time as creating your fabric. By increasing you can make the fabric wider and by decreasing you can make it narrower. There are various techniques you can adopt to achieve the required shape, and the patterns in this book give specific instructions. You will find many of these techniques have already been introduced in earlier sections of this chapter, as the principles of decreasing and increasing can also be used to create lace, bobbles and cable patterning.

Increasing

There are many ways to increase the width of your fabric. Increasing is usually done on the right side of the work and can sometimes be used for decorative purposes as well as to widen your fabric.

Bar increase

Knitting into the front and back of a stitch is a commonly used increasing technique. It is neat and makes a little bar on the right side of the work at the base of the new stitch. This technique can be worked on the first and second-to-last stitch of an increase row.

Alternatively, sometimes a pattern will instruct you to work a few stitches first before the increase, and work to a few stitches before the end of the row and then work the increase so the little bar detail becomes a feature.

1 Work to where the extra stitch is needed. Knit into the front of the next stitch on the left knitting needle without slipping it off.

2 With the stitch still on the left needle and the yarn at the back, knit into the back of the stitch and slip it from the needle.

An increase made by knitting into the front and the back of the stitch.

Eyelet increase

This increase uses the yarn over technique often used in lace knitting and is perhaps the simplest way to increase stitches. It will create a small hole so it is often best used indented a few stitches in from the edge of the fabric so that it becomes a decorative feature as well as a method of shaping the fabric.

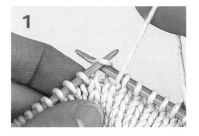

1 Work to where the extra stitch is needed. Bring the yarn forward between both needles, take it over the right needle and hold at the back. Knit the next stitch. Work in pattern to the end of the row.

2 On the next row, purl into the loop as if it were a normal stitch and continue in pattern to the end of the row.

An eyelet increase worked between two stitches.

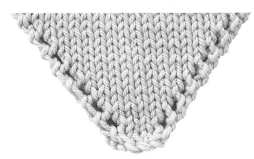

Decreasing

Decreasing can be done on the right or wrong side of the fabric. It involves techniques that allow you to decrease to the right and left so that your decrease shaping looks balanced.

Decreasing to create a slope to the right

This decrease is most commonly achieved by working two or more stitches together. In this shaping the second stitch sits on top of the first stitch to create an effect of the work sloping to the right. This decrease can be worked at the edge of a fabric but can often be used indented at the end of a row by a number of stitches to make it more of a feature.

1 Put the right knitting needle up through the second and then the first stitches on the left needle.

2 Knit the two stitches together and slide both from the left needle.

The stitches create a slope to the right.

Decreasing to create a slope to the left

This form of decrease is used to imitate and mirror the right slope decrease. It is achieved by slipping a stitch, knitting a stitch and then lifting the slipped stitch over the knit stitch. Thus making a shaping detail with the first stitch lying on top of the second stitch. Again, this decrease is often worked in a number of stitches from the edge to mirror the decrease at the end of the row.

1 Slip the first stitch by placing the right needle through it as if knitting, and slide from the left needle.

2 Knit the next stitch.

3 Using the left needle, pass the slipped stitch on the right needle over the top of the knitted stitch. Work to the end of the row.

Joining and Making Up

Blocking and steaming

Blocking your finished knitting before sewing up is an important stage in the construction process and will make an enormous difference to the finished garment. Always check the ball band for yarn care and test a sample first before applying heat to your finished knitting. Pin each piece out to size on a padded board with the wrong side facing you, using a tape-measure to check the measurements. Do not be tempted to skip this measuring stage. It is easy to pull your knitting into the wrong shape without realising it and surprising how much fabric can be steamed into the correct shape if required.

Lay a dampened cotton cloth on top of the knitted fabric, and gently apply the iron. Avoiding stamping the iron too heavily or pushing it along the fabric surface. If the yarn is very delicate, or the fabric highly textured, pin out the pieces, mist them with a water spray and allow them to dry naturally.

Making up

The making up process is generally the same for the majority of garments in this book and any special instructions will be mentioned at the end of each individual pattern.

The step-by-step instructions for joining will demonstrate how to attach your knitted pieces together. This is an important stage in the finishing process and can help you achieve a professional finish.

Invisible seam with mattress stitch

This technique is worked with right sides facing you and allows you to check that you are working in line with the corresponding rows and stitches on both knitted pieces so that the seam looks as neat and unnoticeable as possible.

1 It is important to get a neat edge when joining seams. To achieve this, lay out the two edges which need seaming together, with right sides facing you and seam edges vertical to you. Thread a sewing needle with yarn and bring it through from the back as close to the bottom edge and side as possible. Make a figure of eight as illustrated. This gives a neat start to the seam.

2 Having taken the yarn through the right fabric piece, take the needle across and under the left piece of fabric and up through the same hole as the yarn creating the figure of eight.

3 From the front, insert the needle into the side of the next stitch up on the right-hand side. Pointing the needle up, bring it through to the front, so that two bars of yarn lie across the needle.

4 Take the needle across to the left-hand side and insert it into the stitch that the last stitch left from. Pointing the needle up, bring it through to the front, two stitches up. Work like this from side to side pulling up the stitches every 2.5 cm (1 in) to tighten the seam.

TEXTURED KNITS

Joining the sleeve to the body with mattress stitch

This technique is worked with right sides facing you and allows you to check that you are working in line with the corresponding rows and stitches on both knitted pieces so that the seam looks as neat and unnoticeable as possible.

When joining a sleeve to the body, mark the centre of the sleeve with a pin and match up to the shoulder seam. Hold with a tacking stitch. Do the same at the points where the sleeves meet the side edge of the armhole.

1 Following the instruction for mattress stitch on page 41, stitch in one stitch on the body and as close to the cast-off edge as possible on the sleeve. Bring the sewing needle through the centre of the edge stitch on the sleeve. From the front, insert the needle in between two stitches on the body and bring it through to the front of the work two bars up.

2 From the front, insert the needle back into the stitch on the sleeve that the yarn started from, and keeping the needle horizontal, come through the work two bars along to the left.

3 Continue to work in this way, but take three bars from the body every couple of stitches. This will make sure that the body and sleeve fit together evenly without stretching.

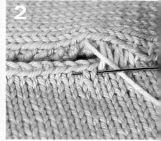

Grafting

This can be a useful technique when needing an invisible seam and when two fabrics are still on the needles.

1 Using the knitting yarn, work from right to left. From the back of the fabric, bring the needle through the first knitted stitch of the lower fabric, and through the first stitch of the upper fabric.

2 From the front, thread the needle back through the centre of the first stitch on the lower fabric where the yarn leaves, then out of the centre of the next stitch on the left.

3 Thread the needle through the centre of the top stitch and along the centre of the next. Continue like this and as each stitch is worked, keep slipping the knitting needle from it.

Picking up stitches

This technique is most commonly used for neck bands and provides a seamless finish. It involves picking up a certain number of stitches at specified points of the neck to give an even finish. These instructions are written into each pattern as they are particular to each project.

1 Holding the needle in your right hand, insert it through the centre of the first stitch from the front to the back.

2 Wrap the new piece of yarn around the knitting needle from back to front, as if to knit.

3 Pull the loop through the knitted stitch to the front.

When picking up stitches on a vertical edge, such as down the front or back of the neck, use this same method but pick up one stitch in from the edge. Depending on the pattern instructions, not every stitch will be required, so pick up stitches as evenly as possible to avoid stretching certain areas.

Attaching collars

1 To attach a collar evenly and neatly, fold it in half, or count the knitted stitches to find the centre. Pin this point to the centre back neck and join together with a tacking stitch. Repeat this with the front edges each side.

2 To sew the collar to the body, thread a needle with enough yarn to sew the whole seam. Start at the centre back. Bring half the length of yarn through and begin to sew the collar to the neck using a slip stitch or mattress stitch. When you have reached the centre front, secure the yarn on the inside edge. Then return to the centre back to stitch the remaining side.

COSY KNITS

This section includes a collection of easy starter projects, using simple techniques and warm, brushed, comforting yarns.

A collection of tactile surfaces in comfortable shapes has been created: items that you will want to wear when curled up in front of the TV, or on the days when you want to feel warm indoors. Textures include simple garter stitch, easy lengthened stitch, and knit and purl patterns that bring the yarn to life.

PROJECT 1:
Scarf and Hat

The scarf is an excellent starter project, and uses a combination of yarns to achieve lots of textural interest. Both projects are knitted on larger needles and use a simple stitch to achieve quick and easy results.

Materials

Yarn A: 2 x 50 g balls Rowan Kid Classic, Shade 833/70% lambswool, 26% kid mohair and 4% nylon, bright pink (approx 140 m (151 yd) per 50 g (1¾ oz) ball)

Yarn B: 1 x 50 g ball Jaeger Extra Fine Merino DK, Shade 985/Merino wool DK, scarlet (approx 125 m (137 yd) per 50 g (1¾ oz) ball)

Yarn C: 1 x 50 g ball Rowan Wool Cotton, Shade 953/50:50 wool:cotton DK mix, blue (approx 113 m (124 yd) per 50 g (1¾ oz) ball)

Yarn D: 2 x 50 g balls Jaeger Extra Fine Merino DK, Shade 931/Merino wool DK, cream (approx 125 m (137 yd) per 50 g (1¾ oz) ball)

Needles: 6 mm (size 10) and 5.5 mm (size 9)

Check your tension

14 sts x 20 rows to 10 x 10 cm (4 x 4 in) measured over garter stitch using 6 mm (size 10) needles and yarns A and C together.

Abbreviations

See page 16.

Hat

Cast on 78 sts using 5.5 mm (size 9) needles using yarns A and B together.

Work in garter stitch for 4 rows.

Change to 6 mm (size 10) needles and work as follows:

Rows 5-24: Using yarns A and C work in garter stitch.

Row 25: (RS) k8 *sl 1, k1, psso, k1, k2tog, k14, repeat from * twice, sl 1, k1, psso, k1, k2tog, k8.

Row 26: (WS) k9 *p1, k16, repeat from * twice, p1, k9.

Row 27: (RS) k7 *sl 1, k1, psso, k1, k2tog, k12, repeat from * twice, sl 1, k1, psso, k2tog, k7.

Row 28: (WS) k8 *p1, k14, repeat from * twice, p1, k8.

Continue to work as set until 17 sts on needle.

Making up

Thread yarn back through sts and draw together and secure. Sew up back seam.

Make pompom using yarns A, B and D. Attach to centre of hat.

Size

Scarf: 148 x 10 cm (58¼ x 3¹⁵⁄₁₆ in) (without tassels)

Hat: One size

Scarf

Cast on 14 sts using 5.5 mm (size 9) needles using yarns A and C together.

Work in garter stitch for 4 rows.

Change to 6 mm (size 10) needles and work a further 8 rows.

Change to yarns A and B and work for 36 rows.

Change to yarns A and D and work for 200 rows.

Change to yarns A and B and work for 36 rows.

Change to yarns A and C and work for 8 rows.

Change to 5.5 mm (size 9) needles, then complete final 4 rows.

Cast off.

Making up

Sew in loose ends.

Make tassels using 3 strands of yarn D, 1 strand of yarn A, and 1 strand of yarn B for each tassel.

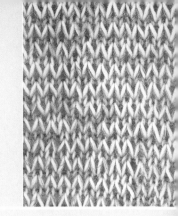

PROJECT 2:
Cosy Sweater

This sweater combines a variety of yarns including mohair to create an unusual visual and tactile contrast. The lengthened stocking stitch pattern is easy to knit and creates elongated stitches so each yarn can behave as it wants. The simple stitch allows you to concentrate on achieving a fantastic shape using the easy shaping instructions in the Basic Skills section.

Materials

Yarn: 4 (4, 5) x 50 g balls Jaeger Extra Fine merino DK, Shade 931/Merino wool DK, cream (approx 125 m (137 yd) per 50 g (1¾ oz) ball) 2 (2, 3) x 25 g balls each Rowan Kidsilk Haze, Shades 604 and 600/Mohair silk mix, caramel and dusty pink (approx 210 m (229 yd) per 25 g (1 oz) ball)

Needles: 6 mm (size 10)

Check your tension

10 sts x 12.5 rows to 10 x 10 cm (4 x 4 in) measured over stitch pattern using 6 mm (size 10) needles.

Abbreviations

See page 16.

Sizes

	Small	Medium	Large
To fit bust cm (in)	86 (34)	91 (36)	97 (38)
Actual size	91 (36)	97 (38)	102 (40)
Back length	62 (24½)	62 (24½)	62 (24½)
Sleeve underarm	48 (19)	48 (19)	48 (19)

Front

Cast on 50 (54, 58) sts using 6 mm (size 10) needles and one strand of each yarn (3 strands).

Work 4 rows in stocking stitch starting with a knit row. Then work in stitch pattern as follows:

Row 5: (RS) k1 (winding yarn around needle twice), repeat to end of row (100 (108, 116) sts on needle).

Row 6: p1, let second stitch (loop stitch) fall off, repeat to end of row (50 (54, 58) sts on needle).

Rows 5-6 form pattern. Repeat throughout.

Rows 7-50: Work in pattern.

Large size only: Work 2 more rows and add 2 to row total from this point.

Shape armhole

Row 51: Cast off 1 st, pattern to end.

Row 52: Cast off 1 st, pattern to end.

Rows 53-58: Repeat rows 51-52 until 42 (46, 50) sts on needle.

Divide for front neck

Row 59: Work 21 (23, 25) sts in pattern, then place remaining sts on holder, turn to work left side of neck.

Rows 60-82: Work in pattern.

Shape shoulder and neck
Row 83: Cast off 4 (5, 6) sts, pattern to end.
Row 84: Pattern.
Rows 85-86: Repeat rows 83-84.
Row 87: Cast off 5 (5, 5) sts at beginning of row (8 sts on needle).
Rows 88-99: Pattern.
Row 100: Cast off.

To work right side of neck
Rejoin yarn and work as for left side, reversing all shaping.

Back
Work as for front until completion of row 58 (row 60 for large size).
Rows 59-82: Pattern.

Shape shoulder and neck
Rows 83-86: Cast off 4 (5, 6) sts, pattern to end.
Rows 87-88: Cast off 5 (5, 5) sts, pattern to end (16 sts on needle).
Row 89: Cast off.

Sleeves - knit two
Cast on 26 (28, 30) sts using 6 mm (size 10) needles and one strand of each yarn (3 strands). Work in stocking stitch for 4 rows.
Rows 5-62: Work in stitch pattern as for back and front. At the same time shape sleeve as follows on rows 15, 25, 35 and 45 until 34 (36, 38) sts on needle.

Shape sleeve
Shaping row: k1, knit into front and back of next st, work in pattern to last st, knit into front and back of it.

Shape sleeve head
Rows 63-64: Cast off 2 (3, 3) sts, pattern to end.
Rows 65-78: Cast off 1 st, pattern to end until 14 (14, 16) sts on needle.
Row 79: Cast off.

Making up
Block and steam all pieces carefully.
Using mattress stitch, join the front to back at shoulders and attach sleeves to body, easing the sleeves into armhole.

Join front neck bands together at cast-off edge to form centre back seam, then ease and stitch front neck band to back of neck to form the collar.
Join the side seams of back and front body and underarm sleeve seams.

PROJECT 3:
Wraparound Cardigan

This garment is a warm and comfortable necessity. It uses a stocking stitch background with flecks of purl stitch to enable the textured yarn to take on its own personality. Its collar, turn back cuffs and long tie-belt in mosaic stitch also give it extra texture and appeal.

Materials
Yarn: 8 (8, 8) x 100 g balls Rowan Polar, Shade 641/Chunky wool blend, red (approx 100 m (109 yd) per 100 g (3½ oz) ball)
Needles: 8 mm (size 11) and 7 mm (size 10½)

Check your tension
12 sts x 16 rows to 10 x 10 cm (4 x 4 in) measured over stocking stitch using 8 mm (size 11) needles.

Abbreviations
See page 16.

Sizes

	Small	Medium	Large
To fit bust cm (in)	86 (34)	92 (36)	96 (38)
Actual size	90 (35½)	94 (37)	103 (40½)
Back length	55 (21½)	55 (21½)	55 (21½)
Sleeve underarm	47 (18½)	47 (18½)	47 (18½)

Left front
Cast on 35 (38, 41) sts using 7 mm (size 10½) needles and work as follows:
Rows 1-12: Work following the hem stitch pattern on the chart for Left Front.
Change to 8 mm (size 11) needles.
Rows 13-41: Work in stitch pattern following the graph, at the same time shape body as follows:
Rows 29 and 41: Cast off 1 st at beginning of row and work in pattern to end until 33 (36, 39) sts on needle.
Rows 42-52: Work without shaping in pattern.
Row 53: Cast off 2 sts, work to end.
Row 54: Work in pattern to end.
Rows 55-62: Cast off 1 st, work to end until 23 (26, 29) sts on needle.
Rows 63-82: Cast off 1 st at beginning of WS rows (neck edge) until 13 (16, 19) sts on needle.
Rows 83-86: Work without shaping in pattern.

Shape shoulder
Row 87: (RS) Cast off 4 (5, 6) sts, work to end.
Row 88: Work in pattern.
Rows 89-90: Repeat rows 87-88 until 5 (6, 7) sts on needle.
Row 91: Cast off.

Right front
Work as for left front but work stitch repeat from Right Front chart and reverse all shaping to alternate sides.

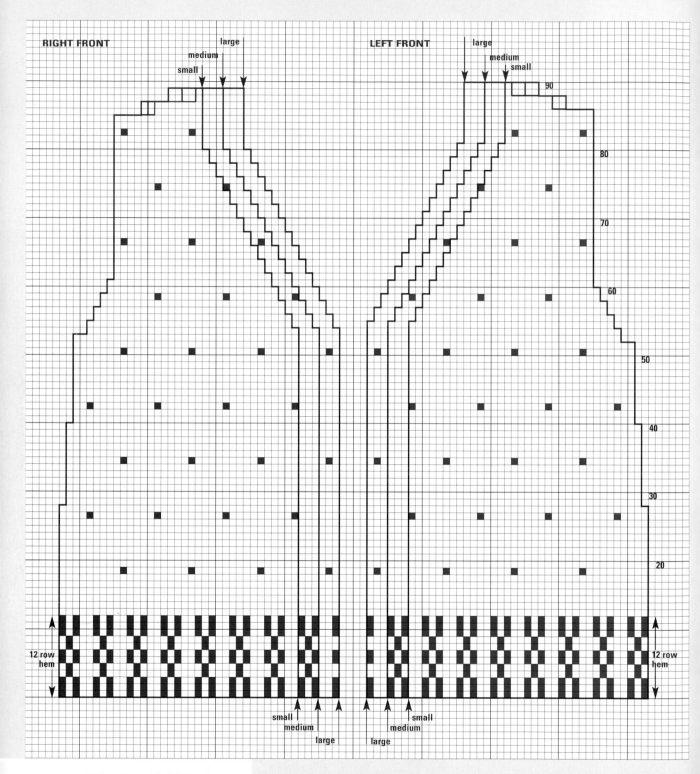

Key to charts:

☐ k on RS, p on WS

■ p on RS, k on WS

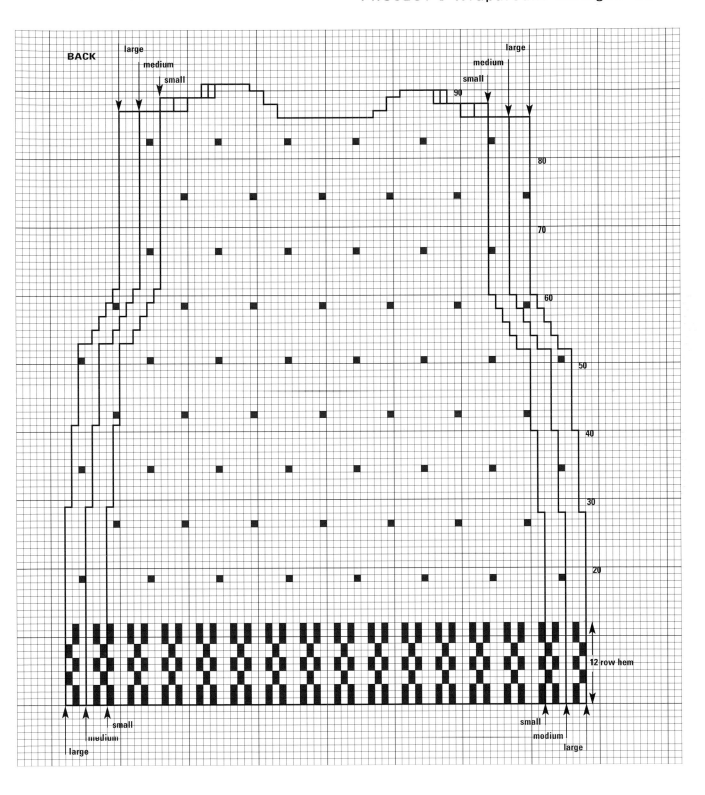

BACK

large
medium
small

large
medium
small

90

80

70

60

50

40

30

20

12 row hem

small
medium
large

small
medium
large

Back

Rows 1-12: Cast on 64 (70, 76) sts using 7 mm (size 10½) needles. Work following the hem stitch pattern on chart.

Change to 8 mm (size 11) needles.

Rows 13-42: Work in stitch pattern following the chart. At the same time shape body as follows:

Row 29: (RS) Cast off 1 st, work in pattern to end.

Row 30: Cast off 1 st, work to end.

Rows 41-42: Repeat rows 29-30 until 60 (66,72) sts on needle.

Rows 43-52: Work without shaping.

Shape armhole

Rows 53-54: RS facing. Cast off 2 sts, pattern to end.

Rows 55-62: Cast off 1 st, pattern to end until 48 (54, 60) sts on needle.

Rows 63-86: Work without shaping in pattern.

Shape neck and shoulder

Row 87: (RS) Cast off 4 (5, 6) sts, pattern 13 (15, 17) sts, then place remaining sts on a holder, turn to work right side of neck.

Row 88: (WS) Cast off 2 sts, work to end.

Row 89: (RS) Cast off 4 (5, 6) sts, work to end.

Row 90: Repeat row 88 (5 (6, 7) sts on needle).

Row 91: Cast off.

To work left side of neck

Rejoin yarn and cast off 14 sts. Then work in pattern to end of row and work as for right side reversing all shaping.

Sleeves – knit two

Cast on 30 (32, 34) sts using 7 mm (size 10½) needles.

Rows 1-12: Work following the hem stitch pattern on chart.

Change to 8 mm (size 11) needles.

Rows 13-20: Work in stitch pattern following the Sleeve chart. Shape as follows:

Row 21: (RS) Increase 1 st each side as follows: k2, then knit into front and back of next st, work in pattern to last 4 sts, knit into front and back of next st, k3.

Rows 22-61: Repeat this increase row every 8 rows until 42 (44, 46) sts on needle.

Rows 62-76: Work without shaping for 15 rows.

Shape sleeve head

Rows 77-78: RS facing. Cast off 3 (4, 4) sts, work to end.

Rows 79-94: Cast off 1 st, work to end of row until 20 (20, 22) sts on needle.

Row 95: Cast off.

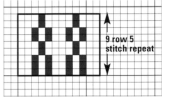

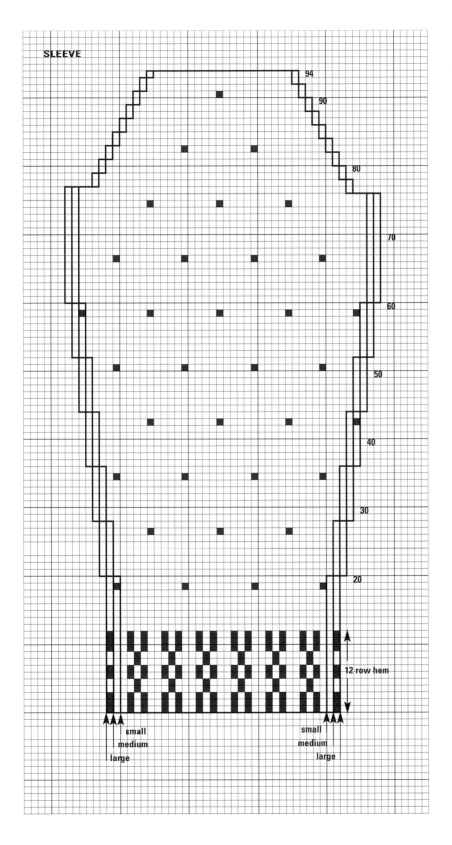

SLEEVE

94

90

80

70

60

50

40

30

20

12 row hem

small
medium
large

small
medium
large

COLLAR/BELT

9 row 5
stitch repeat

Key to charts:

☐ k on RS, p on WS

■ p on RS, k on WS

Making up

Block and steam all pieces carefully.

Using mattress stitch, join the left and right fronts to back at shoulders and attach sleeves to body, easing the sleeves into armhole. Leave side seams and underarm seams open.

Front bands and collar

Right

Cast on 12 sts using 7 mm (size 10½) needles.

Work 54 rows using the Collar stitch pattern chart.

Row 55: (RS) Work in pattern to last 2 sts, increase 1 by working into the front and back of next st, then work last stitch in pattern.

Rows 56-79: Repeat this increase row every 4th row until 19 sts on needle.

Rows 80-102: Work without shaping.

Row 103: Cast off.

Left

Work as for right side reversing all shaping.

Gently stretch the front bands to fit the front sections so as to achieve a clean edge, and ease collar into place around neck attaching the curved side of collar to the neck edge. Stitch/graft the left and right collar pieces together at back neck.

Join the side seams of back and front body and underarm sleeve seams.

Belt

Cast on 12 sts using 7 mm (size 10½) needles.

Using the stitch pattern chart for the Collar work until belt measures approx 150 cm (60 in) or to required length. Cast off.

PROJECT 4:
Brushed Mohair Scarf

This easy-to-knit scarf uses a combination of mohair brushed stripes and flat areas of merino wool to create a soft and fluffy tactile surface using only the simplest of knit structures.

Materials

Yarn A: 1 x 50 g ball Jaeger Extra Fine Merino DK, Shade 936/Merino wool DK, oatmeal (approx 125 m (137 yd) per 50 g (1¾ oz) ball)

Yarn B: 1 x 25 g ball Rowan Kidsilk Haze, Shade 606/Mohair silk mix, cerise pink (210 m (229 yd) per 25 g (1 oz) ball)

Split ball to use 2 strands together

Yarn C: 1 x 25 g ball Rowan Kidsilk Haze, Shade 604/Mohair silk mix, caramel (210 m (229 yd) per 25 g (1 oz) ball)

Split ball to use 2 strands together

Needles: 4 mm (size 6)

Other: 1 mohair brush

Check your tension

22 sts x 30 rows to 10 x 10 cm (4 x 4 in) measured over stocking stitch using 4 mm (size 6) needles.

Scarf

Cast on 176 sts using 4 mm (size 6) needles and yarn A.

Work in stocking stitch throughout starting with a knit row.

Work 2 rows in yarn A.

Change to yarn B and work for 2 rows.
Change to yarn C and work for 10 rows.
Change to yarn A and work for 4 rows.
Change to yarn B and work for 18 rows.
Change to yarn A and work for 10 rows.
Change to yarn C and work for 10 rows.
Change to yarn B and work for 4 rows.
Cast off.

*With right side facing, pick up 44 sts evenly along one of the side ends of the scarf fabric using yarn B.

Starting with a purl row work in stocking stitch as follows:
Work 36 rows in yarn B.
Change to yarn A and work for 8 rows.
Change to yarn C and work for 12 rows.
Change to yarn B and work for 4 rows.
Cast off.

Then turn to the other side end of the scarf fabric and work from * as before.

Finishing

Sew in all loose ends.

Using a mohair brush, brush the mohair sections of the central panel of the scarf (in the direction of cast-off edge to cast-on edge) to raise the pile of the yarn.

Then do the same at either end of the scarf sections.

Measure out and then press lightly to control the surface texture of the fabric.

Size

120 x 20 cm (47 x 8 in)

PROJECT 5:
Easy-knit Socks

These socks are wonderfully warm and would be a great complementary accessory or an ideal gift idea. They are knitted using a soft, cosy yarn and have a bobble stitch trim at the top.

Materials
Yarn: 1 x 50 g ball Rowan Kid Classic, Shade 833/70% lambswool, 26% kid mohair and 4% nylon, pink (approx 140 m (151 yd) per 50 g (1¾ oz) ball)
Needles: 5 mm (size 8) and 4 mm (size 6)

Check your tension
19 sts x 25 rows to 10 x 10 cm (4 x 4 in) measured over stocking stitch using 5 mm (size 8) needles.

Abbreviations
See page 16.

Special abbreviations
MB – (k1, p1, k1, p1, k1) into next stitch, turn, k5, turn and k5tog.

Left sock
Cast on 40 sts using 4 mm (size 6) needles.
Row 1: (RS) *k1, p1, repeat from * to end.
Row 2: *k1, p1, repeat from * to end.
Row 3: k1 *p1, MB, p1, k1, repeat from * to last 3 sts, p1, k1, p1.

Row 4: Repeat row 2.
Row 5: k1, p1, k1 *p1, MB, p1, k1, repeat from * to last st, p1.
Rows 6-14: Work in rib.
Rows 15-27: Change to 5 mm (size 8) needles. Work in stocking st.

Shape heel
Row 28: (WS) p20, then turn.
Row 29: k19, turn.
Row 30: p18, turn.
Rows 31-40: Work as set until p8 has been reached.
Row 41: (RS) k9, turn.
Row 42: p10, turn.
Row 43: k11, turn.
Rows 44-52: Work as set until p20 has been reached.
Rows 53-88: Work in stocking st across all sts.

Shape toe
Row 89: (RS) k1, sl 1, k1, psso, k14, k2tog, k1, sl 1, k1, psso, k14, k2tog, k1.
Row 90: Purl.
Row 91: k1, sl 1, k1, psso, k12, k2tog, k1, sl 1, k1, psso, k12, k2tog, k1.
Row 92: Purl
Rows 93-96: Work as set.
Row 97: k1, sl 1, k1, psso, k6, k2tog, k1, sl 1, k1, psso, k6, k2tog, k1.
Row 98: Purl.
Row 99: Cast off.

Size
To fit size 4-8

Right sock

Cast on 40 sts using 4 mm (size 6) needles.

Row 1: (RS) *k1, p1, repeat from * to end.

Row 2: k1, p1, repeat from * to end.

Row 3: k1, p1, k1 *p1, MB, p1, k1, repeat from * to last st, p1.

Row 4: As row 2.

Row 5: k1 *p1, MB, p1, k1, repeat from * to last 3 sts, p1, k1, p1.

Rows 6-14: Work in rib.

Rows 15-28: Change to 5 mm (size 8) needles. Work in stocking st.

Shape heel

Row 29: (RS) k20, turn.

Row 30: p19, turn.

Row 31: k18, turn.

Rows 32-41: Work as set until k8 has been reached.

Row 42: p9, turn.

Row 43: k10, turn.

Row 44: p11, turn.

Rows 45-52: Work as set until p19 has been reached.

Rows 53-88: Work in stocking st across all sts.

Shape toe

Row 89: (RS) k1, sl 1, k1, psso, k14, k2tog, k1, sl 1, k1, psso, k14, k2tog, k1.

Row 90: Purl.

Row 91: k1, sl 1, k1, psso, k12, k2tog, k1, sl 1, k1, psso, k12, k2tog, k1.

Row 92: Purl

Rows 93-96: Work as set.

Row 97: k1, sl 1, k1, psso, k6, k2tog, k1, sl 1, k1, psso, k6, k2tog, k1.

Row 98: Purl.

Row 99: Cast off.

Making up

Stitch along toe and side seam using mattress stitch, and sew in any loose ends.

LINEAR KNITS

This section features contemporary, simple shapes using refined knit surfaces. A combination of knit and purl stitch patterns have been created using clean, smooth yarns to make the most of diagonal rib and linear stitch textures.

PROJECT 6:
Skinny-rib Cardigan

This useful cardigan uses a smooth yarn to allow the qualities of the two by two rib stitch pattern come to life. The use of simple shaping techniques also helps to enhance the linear textured effect.

Materials

Yarn: 10 (10, 11) x 50 g balls Rowan Wool Cotton Shade 933/50:50 wool:cotton DK mix, violet (approx 113 m (124 yd) per 50 g (1¾ oz) ball)

Needles: 4 mm (size 6) and 3.75 mm (size 5)

Other: 6 buttons

Check your tension

22 sts x 30 rows to 10 x 10 cm (4 x 4 in) measured over stocking stitch using 4 mm (size 6) needles.

Abbreviations

See page 16.

Note: Avoid joining yarn on neck edge or button edges as this will form the finished edge.

Sizes

	Small	Medium	Large
To fit bust cm (in)	86 (34)	91 (36)	97 (38)
Actual size	91 (36)	97 (38)	102 (40)
Back length	55 (22)	55 (22)	55 (22)
Sleeve underarm	48 (19)	48 (19)	48 (19)

Left front

Cast on 54 (62,70) sts using 3.75 mm (size 5) needles, and work as follows:

Rows 1-6: Work in k2, p2, rib.

Rows 7-24: Work in p2, k2, rib.

Change to 4 mm (size 6) needles and work body as follows:

Rows 1-68: Work in k2, p2, rib.

Shape armhole

Row 69: (RS) Cast off 2 sts, work in rib to end.

Row 70: (WS) Work in rib to end.

Row 71: (RS) p2, k1, sl 1, k1, psso, rib to end.

Rows 72-83: Repeat rows 70-71 six times until 45 (53, 61) sts on needle.

Row 84: Work in rib to end.

Shape neck

Row 85: (RS) p2, k1, sl 1, k1, psso, work in rib to last 7 sts, k2tog, k1, p2, k2.

Row 86: Work in rib to end.

Row 87: Work in rib to last 7 sts, k2tog, k1, p2, k2.

Row 88-103: Repeat rows 86-87 eight times until 34 (42, 50) sts on needle.

Rows 104-127: Work row 87 every other RS row (every 4th row) until neck shaping complete (28 (36, 44) sts on needle).

Rows 128-134: Work in rib.

Medium size: Work 2 more rows (136 rows).

Large size: Work 4 more rows (138 rows).

Shape shoulder

Next row: (RS) Cast off 6 (8, 10) sts at beginning of row and next 2 RS rows until 10 (12, 14) sts on needle.

Work 1 row. Cast off in rib.

Button marking

Mark position for 6 buttons, the first 18 rows from bottom edge, and the last 4 rows from top edge where neck shaping begins. Place the remaining buttons evenly spaced between the first and last.

Buttonholes

On the right front work buttonholes to match marked button positions on left front. Make buttonholes as follows:

Row 1: (RS) k2, p2tog, rib to end.

Row 2: (WS) Rib to last 3 sts, yo, k1, p2.

Right front

Cast on 54 (62, 70) sts using 3.75 mm (size 5) needles, and work as follows. Note that buttonholes are to be worked at same time.

Rows 1-6: Work in k2, p2, rib.

Rows 7-24: Work in p2, k2, rib.

Change to 4 mm (size 6) needles and work body as follows:

Rows 1-69: Work in k2, p2, rib.

Shape armhole

Row 70: (WS) Cast off 2 sts, work in rib to end.

Row 71: (RS) Work in rib to last 5 sts, k2tog, k1, p2.

Row 72: Work in rib.

Rows 73-84: Repeat rows 71-72 six times until 45 (53, 61) sts on needle.

Shape neck

Row 85: (RS) k2, p2, k1, sl 1, k1, psso, rib to last 5 sts, k2tog, k1, p2.

Row 86: Work in rib.

Row 87: k2, p2, k1, sl 1, k1, psso, rib to end.

Rows 88-103: Repeat rows 86-87 eight times until 34 (42, 50) sts on needle.

Rows 104-127: Work row 87 every other RS row (every 4th row) until the neck shaping is complete (28 (36, 44) sts on needle).

Rows 128-135: Work in rib.

Medium size: Work 2 more rows (137 rows).

Large size: Work 4 more rows (139 rows).

Shape shoulder

Next row: (WS) Cast off 6 (8, 10) sts at beginning of row and next 2 WS rows until 10 (12, 14) sts on needle.

Work 1 row. Cast off in rib.

Back

Cast on 108 (118, 128) sts using 3.75 mm (size 5) needles, and work as follows:

Rows 1-6: Work in k2, p2, rib.

Rows 7-24: Work in p2, k2, rib.

Change to 4 mm (size 6) needles and work body as follows:

Rows 1-68: Work in k2, p2, rib.

Shape armhole

Rows 69-70: Cast off 2 sts, work in rib to end.

Row 71: (RS) p2, k1, sl 1, k1, psso, rib to last 5 sts, k2tog, k1, p2.

Row 72: Rib to end.

Rows 73-86: Repeat rows 71-72 seven times until 88 (98, 108) sts on needle.

Rows 87-134: Work in rib.

Medium size: Work 2 more rows (136 rows).

Large size: Work 4 more rows (138 rows).

Shape shoulder and back neck:

Next row: (RS) Cast off 6 (8, 10) sts, rib 20 (23, 26) sts, k2tog, k1, p2. Place remaining sts on holder. Turn to work right side of back neck.

Next row: (WS) Rib to end.

Next row: (RS) Cast off 6 (8, 9) sts, rib to last 5 sts, k2tog, k1, p2.

Repeat this last row on next RS row to continue shaping neck and shoulder edge until 10 (9, 10) sts on needle.

Work 1 row.

Cast off.

To work left side of neck

(RS) Rejoin yarn and cast off 26 sts, p2, k1, sl 1, k1, psso, rib to end.

Next row: (WS) Cast off 6 (8, 10) sts, rib to end.

Next row: (RS) p2, k1, sl 1, k1, psso, rib to end.

Next row: (WS) Cast off 6 (8, 9) sts, rib to end.

Repeat last 2 rows to continue shaping on neck and shoulder until 10 (9, 10) sts on needle.

Work 1 row.

Cast off in rib.

Sleeves - knit two

Cast on 54 (58, 62) sts using 3.75 mm (size 5) needles, and
    work as follows:

Rows 1-6: Work in k2, p2, rib.

Rows 7-24: Work in p2, k2, rib.

Change to 4 mm (size 6) needles and work sleeve as follows:

Rows 1-26: Work in k2, p2 rib.

Shape sleeve

Row 27: (RS) Inc one stitch at the beginning and end of row.

Rows 28-107: Repeat this inc row every 10 rows until 72
    (76, 80) sts on needle.

Rows 108-122: Work without shaping in rib.

Shape sleeve head

Rows 123-124: Cast off 3 sts, rib to end.

Row 125: (RS) Dec 2 sts each side by, k2, p2, k1, sl 1, k1,
    psso, k2tog, k1, rib to last 9 sts, sl 1, p2tog, psso, k2, p2, k2.

Row 126: (WS) Rib to end.

Row 127: (RS) Dec 1 st each side by, k2, p2, k1, sl 1, k1,
    psso, work in rib to last 7 sts, k2tog, k1,p2, k2.

Rows 128-161: Repeat rows 126-127 seventeen times
    until 26 (30, 34) sts on needle.

Row 162: Rib to end.

Row 163: Cast off in rib.

Making up

Block and steam all pieces carefully.

Using mattress stitch, join the left and right front to back
    at shoulders and attach sleeves to body, easing the
    sleeve head into the armhole. Join side seams and
    underarm seams using mattress stitch.

Sew on buttons.

This cardigan has no collar, so a back neck facing is
    required to give a neat finish. Cast on 5 sts using 3.75
    mm (size 5) needles. Work in stocking stitch until facing
    fits back neck when slightly stretched. Cast off, then
    slip stitch in place.

PROJECT 7:
Stitch-effect Sweater

This project uses knit and purl stitch combinations to create flattering optical and grid-like patterns. This is a stylish, easy sweater that has great visual impact.

Materials
Yarn: 9 (9, 10) x 50 g balls Jaeger Extra Fine Merino DK, Shade 941/Merino wool DK, grey (approx 125 m (137 yd) per 50 g (1¾ oz) ball)
Needles: 4 mm (size 6) and 3.75 mm (size 5)

Check your tension
22 sts x 30 rows to 10 x 10 cm (4 x 4 in) measured over stocking stitch using 4 mm (size 6) needles.

Abbreviations
See page 16.

Front
Cast on 100 (104, 112) sts using 3.75 mm (size 5) needles and work as follows:
Row 1: (RS) k2, *p1, k3, repeat from * to last 2 sts, p1, k1.
Row 2: (WS) p1, *k1, p3, repeat from * to last 3 sts, k1, p2.
Rows 3-8: Repeat rows 1-2 three times.
Medium size only: Inc each end of last row.
(100 (106, 112) sts on needle.)
Change to 4 mm (size 6) needles and work main body as follows:
Rows 1-86: Work in pattern following the stitch chart for Front.

Shape armhole
Rows 87-88: Cast off 2 sts, pattern to end.
Rows 89-100: Cast off 1 st, pattern to end until 84 (90, 96) sts on needle.
Rows 101-140: Work without shaping.

Shape neck
Row 141: (RS) Work 28 (31, 34) sts in pattern, place remaining sts on a holder, and turn to work left side of neck.
Row 142: (WS) Work in pattern to end.
Row 143: (RS) Work in pattern to last 6 sts, k3tog, k3.
Rows 144-151: Repeat rows 142-143 four times until 18 (21, 24) sts on needle.
Rows 152-154: Work in pattern.

Sizes

	Small	Medium	Large
To fit bust cm (in)	86 (34)	91 (36)	97 (38)
Actual size	91 (36)	97 (38)	102 (40)
Back length	53 (21)	53 (21)	53 (21)
Sleeve underarm	47 (18½)	47 (18½)	47 (18½)

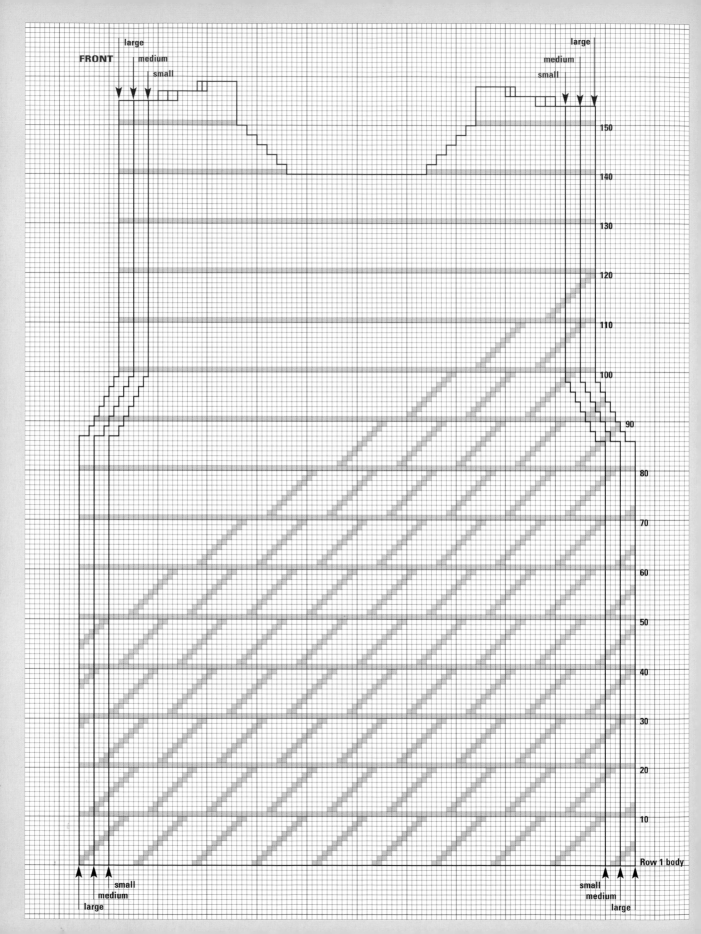

BACK

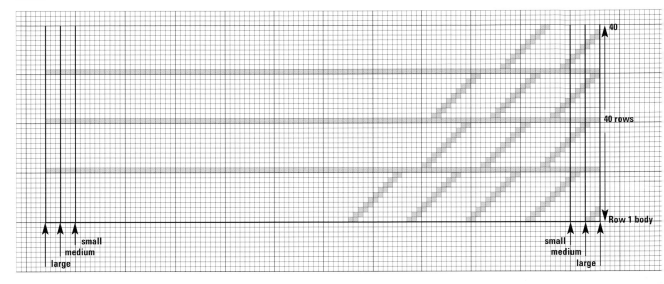

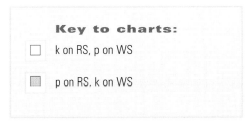

Key to charts:

☐ k on RS, p on WS

▨ p on RS, k on WS

Shape shoulder

Rows 155-157: Cast off 6 (7, 8) sts at beginning of row 155 and next RS row (6 (7, 8) sts on needle).

Row 158: Purl.

Row 159: Cast off.

Work right side of neck

Row 141: (RS) Rejoin yarn and cast off 28 sts. Work in pattern to end.

Row 142: Work in pattern to end.

Row 143: k3, sl 1, k2tog, psso, work in pattern to end.

Rows 144-151: Repeat rows 142-143 four times until 18 (21, 24) sts on needle.

Rows 152-155: Work in pattern.

Shape shoulder

Rows 156-158: Cast off 6 (7, 8) sts at beginning of row 156 and next WS row (6 (7, 8) sts on needle)

Row 159: Knit.

Row 160: Cast off.

Back

Cast on and work hem as for front (100 (106, 112 sts).

Rows 1-40: Work in pattern following the stitch chart for Back.

Row 41: (RS) Purl to end.

Row 42: (WS) Purl to end.

Row 43: (RS) Knit to end.

Row 44-49: Repeat rows 42-43 three times.

Row 50: Purl to end.

Rows 41-50 form the pattern repeat throughout.

Rows 51-86: Work in pattern.

Shape armhole

Rows 87-88: Cast off 2 sts, work in pattern to end.

Rows 89-100: Cast off 1 st at the beginning of each row and work in pattern to end until 84 (90, 96) sts on needle.

Rows 101-150: Work in pattern without shaping.

Shape back neck and shoulder

Row 151: p22 (25, 28), place remaining sts on holder. Turn to work right side of back neck.

Row 152: Purl to end.

Row 153: Knit to last 6 sts, k3tog, k3.

Row 154: Purl to end.

Row 155: Cast off 6 (7, 8) sts, work to last 6 sts, k3tog, k3.

Row 156: Purl to end.

Row 157: Cast off 6 (7, 8) sts, knit to end.

Row 158: Purl to end.

Row 159: Cast off.

To work left side

Row 151: (RS) Rejoin yarn and cast off 40 sts, purl to end.

Row 152: Purl to end.

Row 153: (RS) k3, sl 1, k2tog, psso, knit to end.

Then work as for right side, reversing all shaping.

Sleeves - knit two

Cast on 54 (54, 54) sts using 3.75 mm (size 5) needles and work as follows:

Row 1: (RS) k2 *p1, k3, repeat from * to end.

Row 2: (WS) *p3, k1, repeat from * to last 2 sts, p2.

Rows 3-8: Repeat rows 1-2 three times.

Large size only: Inc each end of last row.

(54, (54, 56) sts on needle.)

Change to 4 mm (size 6) needles.

Work for a total of 26 rows without shaping as follows:

Rows 1-6: Work in stocking stitch.

Row 7: (RS) Purl to end.

Row 8: (WS) Purl to end.

Row 9: (RS) Knit to end.

Rows 10-15: Repeat rows 8-9 three times.

Row 16: Purl to end.

Rows 7-16 form the pattern repeat throughout.

Rows 17-26: Work in pattern.

Shape sleeve

Row 27: (RS) p3, inc 1, purl to last 5 sts, inc 1, p4.

Rows 28-107: Repeat this inc row every 10 rows until 72 (72, 74) sts on needle.

Rows 108-130: Work in pattern without shaping.

Shape sleeve head

Rows 131-132: Cast off 4 sts, pattern to end.

Row 133: (RS) Dec 2 sts each side by: k3, k3tog, sl 1, k2tog, psso, knit to last 6 sts, sl 1, k2tog, psso, k3.

Row 134: Purl to end.

Row 135: k3, k3tog, purl to last 6 sts, sl 1, k2tog, psso, k3.

Row 136: Purl to end.

Row 137: (RS) Dec 1 st each side by: k3, k2tog, pattern to last 5 sts, sl 1, k1, psso, k3.

Row 138: Purl to end.

Rows 139-168: Repeat rows 129-130 fifteen times until 24 (24, 26) sts on needle.

Row 169: Cast off.

Making up

Block and steam all pieces carefully.

Using mattress stitch, join the front to back at right shoulder.

Collar

Using 3.75 mm (size 5) needles, pick up 17 sts down the left front neck shaping, 28 sts across the front neck, 17 sts up the right front neck shaping and 51 sts around back neck (113 sts on needle).

Work 8 rows in rib pattern as for hems. Cast off in stitch repeat.

Using mattress stitch join the left shoulder seam and collar seam. Attach sleeves to body easing the sleeve head into the armhole. Join the side seams and underarm sleeve seams using mattress stitch.

PROJECT 8:
Diagonal-stitch Cardigan

This cardigan is an essential item and can be made with a zip front or without a fastening if you prefer. The combination of knit and purl stitches creates a dramatic and modern appearance to a useful piece, and the yarn is smooth and easy to knit with.

Materials

Yarn: 9 (10, 10) x 50 g balls Rowan All Seasons Cotton, Shade 191/60% cotton:40% acrylic mix, off-white (approx 90 m (98 yd) per 50 g (1¾ oz) ball)

Needles: 4.5 mm (size 7) and 4 mm (size 6)

Other: 50 cm (20 in) open-ended zip

Check your tension

18 sts x 25 rows to 10 x 10 cm (4 x 4 in) measured over stocking stitch using 4.5 mm (size 7) needles.

Abbreviations

See page 16.

Sizes

	Small	Medium	Large
To fit bust cm (in)	86 (34)	91 (36)	97 (38)
Actual size	99 (39)	104 (41)	109 (43)
Back length	53.5 (21½)	53.5 (21½)	53.5 (21½)
Sleeve underarm	47 (18½)	47 (18½)	47 (18½)

Left front

Cast on 40 (44, 48) sts using 4 mm (size 6) needles.

Work 14 rows in k1, p1, rib. (Every row *k1, p1, repeat from * to end.)

Change to 4.5 mm (size 7) needles and work body as follows:

Rows 1-66: Work in pattern following the chart for Left Front. These 14 rows form the stitch pattern repeat and should be kept to sequence throughout.

Shape armhole

Row 67: (RS) Cast off 2 sts, work to end.

Row 68: Work in pattern.

Row 69: Cast off 1 st, work to end.

Rows 70-79: Repeat rows 68-69 four times until 32 (36, 40) sts on needle.

Rows 80-101: Pattern without shaping.

Shape neck

Row 102: (WS) Cast off 2 sts at beginning of row, pattern to end

Row 103: Pattern to end.

Rows 104-113: Repeat rows 102-103 five times until 20 (24, 28) sts on needle.

Rows 114-122: Pattern without shaping.

Shape shoulder

Rows 123-125: (RS) Cast off 6 (8, 9) sts at beginning of row and next RS row (8 (8,10) sts on needle).

Row 126: Pattern to end.

Row 127: Cast off.

BACK

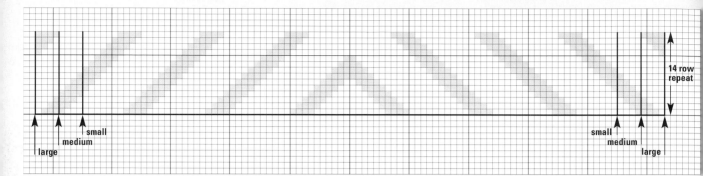

RIGHT FRONT

LEFT FRONT

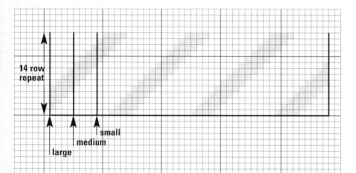

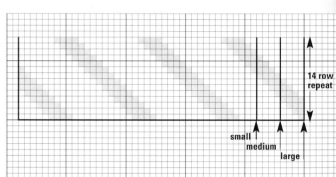

SLEEVES

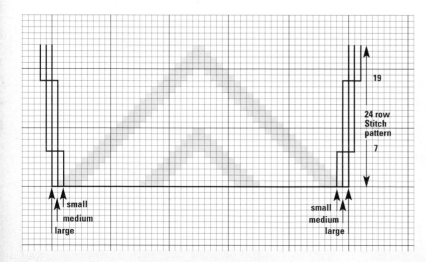

Key to charts:

☐ k on RS, p on WS

▨ p on RS, k on WS

Right front

Work as for left front but work stitch repeat from
Right Front chart and reverse all shaping to
alternate sides.

Back

Cast on 90 (98, 106) sts using 4 mm (size
6) needles and work in k1, p1, rib for
14 rows as for right and left front.
Change to 4.5 mm (size 7) needles
and work body as follows:

Rows 1-66: Work in stitch
pattern following the chart.
This will form the stitch
pattern repeat and
should be kept in
sequence throughout.

Shape armhole
Rows 67-68: Cast off 2 sts, pattern to end.
Rows 69-80: Cast off 1 st, pattern to end until 74 (82, 90) sts on needle.
Rows 81-120: Work in pattern without shaping.

Shape neck and shoulder
Row 121: (RS) Pattern for 24 (28, 32) sts, then place remaining sts on a holder, turn to work right side of neck.
Row 122: Pattern to end.
Row 123: (RS) Cast off 6 (8, 9) sts, pattern to end.
Row 124: (WS) Cast off 2 sts, pattern to end.
Rows 125-126: Repeat rows 123 and 124 (8 (8, 10) sts on needle).
Row 127: Cast off.

To work left side of neck
Row 121: Rejoin yarn and cast off 26 sts. Then work in pattern to end of row and work as for right side reversing all shaping.

Sleeves - knit two
Cast on 46 (48, 50) sts using 4 mm (size 6) needles and work in k1, p1, rib for 14 rows.
Change to 4.5 mm (size 7) needles and work sleeve as follows:
Rows 1-24: Work in pattern following the Sleeve chart. Increase 1 st each side of rows 7 and 19 as follows: k2 sts, then knit into front and back of next st, work in pattern to last 4 sts then knit into front and back of next st, k3. Once these 24 rows have been completed, work in stocking stitch throughout.

Shape sleeve
Rows 29-79: Repeat the increase row every 12 rows until 60 (62, 64) sts on needle.
Rows 80-102: Work without shaping.

Shape sleeve head
Rows 103-104: Cast off 2 (3, 4) sts, work to end.
Rows 105-126: Cast off 1 st, work to end until 34 sts on needle.
Row 127: Cast off.

Making up
Block and steam all pieces carefully.
Using mattress stitch, join the left and right fronts to back at shoulders and attach sleeves to body, easing the sleeves into armhole. Leave side seams and underarm seams open.

Front bands
Left
Cast on 8 sts using 4 mm (size 6) needles.
Row 1: (RS) p5, k1, p1, k1.
Row 2: (WS) p1, k1, p1, k5.
Repeat rows 1-2 until band is long enough to fit left front from bottom hem to beginning of neck shaping when slightly stretched. Break yarn, leave sts on holder.
Right
Work as for left band except reverse pattern. Also, do not cast off, leave sts on holder and do not break yarn as this will be used to complete collar.
Gently stretch the front bands to fit the front sections so as to achieve a clean edge. Join them together using mattress stitch to give a neat finish.

Collar
Using 4 mm (size 6) needles, pattern across the 8 sts from the right-hand band and then pick up 21 sts from the right front neck shaping. Pick up evenly 35 sts around back neck, then pick up 21 sts from left front neck, then pattern across 8 sts from left front band (93 sts on needle).
Work first and last 8 sts as for front bands and the collar in k1, p1, rib pattern for 26 rows. Cast off in stitch repeat.

Join the side seams of back and front body and underarm sleeve seams. Attach zip.

Optional – make two: To add a neat finish to inside of cardigan and cover zip, cast on 4 sts and work in stocking stitch for number of rows required to fit the length of the front bands and collar when strip is gently stretched. Cast off. Then, slip stitch into place covering the backing of zip.

NATURAL KNITS

This section includes natural textures, tweeds and shetland yarns. Comforting, natural materials and rustic yarns have been used; these are uneven and slubbed, but blended to become softer, brushed or felted. The projects have a feeling of the outdoors and introduce relief textures, cable patterns, tuck stitches and more rugged shapes.

PROJECT 9:
Rugged Soft Sweater

This sweater is a versatile garment. It has chunky rib details, collar and cuffs, and is rough to look at but soft to touch. It is an ideal start to this section as it includes some strong textural statements but uses techniques that are easy to master.

Materials

Yarn: 7 (7) x 100 g balls Rowan Polar, Shade 642/Chunky wool blend, light green (approx 100 m (109 yd) per 100 g (3½ oz) ball)

Needles: 8 mm (size 11) and 7 mm (size 10½)

Check your tension

12 sts x 16 rows to 10 x 10 cm (4 x 4 in) measured over stocking stitch using 8 mm (size 11) needles.

Abbreviations

See page 16.

Sizes

	Small/Medium	Medium/Large
To fit bust cm (in)	86-94 (34-37)	97-107 (38-42)
Actual size	104 (42)	122 (48)
Back length	68 (27)	68 (27)
Sleeve underarm	44 (17½)	44 (17½)

Front

Cast on 70 (78) sts using 7mm (size 10½) needles and work as follows:

Row 1: (RS) k2, *p2, k2, rep from * to end.

Row 2: (WS) p2, *k2, p2, rep from * to end.

Row 3: Knit to end.

Row 4: Purl to end.

Row 5: Repeat row 1.

Row 6: Repeat row 2.

Row 7: Purl to end.

Row 8: Knit to end.

Repeat these rows once more (16 rows in total).

Change to 8 mm (size 11) needles and work body in pattern as follows:

Row 1: (RS) k30 (34) sts, work central panel as (p2, k2) twice, p2, then k to end.

Row 2: (WS) p30 (34) sts, work central panel as (k2, p2) twice, k2, then p to end.

Row 3: Knit to end.

Row 4: Purl to end.

Row 5: Repeat row 1.

Row 6: Repeat row 2.

Row 7: k30 (34) sts, work central panel as p10, then k to end.

Row 8: p 30 (34) sts, work central panel as k10, then p to end.

Repeat these 8 rows throughout. Note: the number of sts before and after the central panel will vary depending on shaping instructions.

Shape body

Rows 9-12: Work without shaping.

Row 13: (RS) Dec 1 st each side by k3, k2tog, pattern to last 5 sts, sl 1, k1, psso, k3.

Rows 14-41: Repeat this dec row on rows 27 and 41 until 64 (72) sts on needle.

Rows 42-54: Work straight in pattern.

Shape armhole

Rows 55-56: Cast off 3 sts, pattern to end.

Row 57: (RS) Dec 1 st each side as follows: k3, sl 1, k1, psso, work in pattern to last 5 sts, k2tog, k3.

Row 58: Pattern to end.

Rows 59-64: Repeat rows 57-58 three times until 50 (58) sts on needle.

Divide front neck

Row 65: RS facing. Work 25 (29) sts in pattern (place remaining sts on holder). Turn and work left side.

Rows 66-81: Work without shaping.

Medium/large size: Work two more rows (83 rows), add two to row total from this point.

  Row 82: (WS) Cast off 5 sts then work to end.

Shape neck

Row 83: (RS) Work in pattern to last 5 sts, k2tog, k3.

Row 84: Pattern to end.

Rows 85-92: Repeat rows 83-84 four times until 15 (19) sts on needle.

Shape shoulder

Row 93: RS facing. Cast off 5 (6) sts, pattern to end.

Row 94: Pattern to end.

Rows 95-96: Repeat rows 93-94 (5 (7) sts on needle).

Row 97: Cast off.

Work right side of neck

Row 65: (RS) Rejoin yarn and work as for left side reversing all shaping.

Back

Cast on 70 (78) sts and work as for front until the armhole decreasing has been completed (Row 58 – 50 (58) sts on needle).

Rows 59-90: Work without shaping.

Medium/large size: Work two more rows (92 rows), add two to row total from this point.

Shape back neck and shoulder

Row 91: (RS) k17 (21)sts, place remaining sts on holder. Turn to work right side of back neck.

Row 92: (WS) Purl to end.

Row 93: (RS) Cast off 5 (6) sts, pattern to last 5 sts, k2tog, k3.

Row 94: Purl to end.

Rows 95-96: Repeat rows 93-94 until 5 (7) sts on needle.

Row 97: Cast off.

To work left side

Row 91: (RS) Rejoin yarn and cast off 16 sts, work in pattern to end.

Then work as for right side reversing all shaping.

Sleeves - knit two

Cast on 30 (34) sts using 7 mm (size 10½) needles.

Rows 1-16: Work hem as for front.

Change to 8 mm (size 11) needles and work sleeve as follows. Work 2 rows in stocking stitch.

Shape sleeve

Row 3: (RS) k3, inc 1, work to last 5 sts, inc 1, k4.

Rows 4-39: Repeat inc row every 6 rows until 44 (48) sts on needle.

Rows 40-54: Work without shaping.

Shape sleeve head

Rows 55-56: Cast off 2 sts, work to end.

Row 57: (RS) Dec 1 st each side by: k3, k2tog, work to last 5 sts, sl 1, k1, psso, k3.

Row 58: Work to end.

Rows 59-72: Repeat rows 49-50 seven (eight) times until 24 (26) sts on needle.

Row 73 (75): Cast off.

Making up

Block and steam all pieces carefully. Using mattress stitch, join the front to back at shoulders.

Collar

Using 7 mm (size 10½) needles, pick up the 5 sts from the left front neck and then pick up a further 13 sts from the left front neck shaping. Pick up evenly 20 sts around back neck and then pick up 13 sts from right front neck and 5 sts from right front neck (56 sts on needle).

Use the first and the last 5 sts as the basis for the rib stitch set up for the collar and work for 16 rows. Cast off in stitch repeat.

Attach sleeves to body easing the sleeve head into the armhole. Join the side seams and underarm seam using mattress stitch.

PROJECT 10:
Bobble-stitch Cardigan

Subtle shaping and a feminine neckline, combined with rib and bobble stitch panels on a stocking stitch background, give this cardigan an unusual twist. This garment introduces the bobble technique and illustrates the textural impact a combination of relief stitches can make.

Materials

Yarn: 6 (7, 7) x 50 g hanks Rowan Rowanspun DK, Shade 747/Flecked wool DK, light green (approx 200 m (220 yd) per 50 g (1¾ oz) hank)

Needles: 4 mm (size 6) and 3.75 mm (size 5)

Other: 6 buttons

Check your tension

21 sts x 30 rows to 10 x 10 cm (4 x 4 in) measured over stocking stitch using 4 mm (size 6) needles.

Abbreviations

See page 16.

Sizes

	Small	Medium	Large
To fit bust cm (in)	86 (34)	91 (36)	97 (38)
Actual size	91 (36)	97 (38)	102 (40)
Back length	58 (23½)	58 (23½)	58 (23½)
Sleeve underarm	46 (18)	46 (18)	46 (18)

Left front

Cast on 49 (52, 55) sts using 3.75 mm (size 5) needles.

Work 16 rows in k1, p1, rib.

Change to 4 mm (size 6) needles and work body as follows:

Rows 1-86: Start to work in stitch pattern following the chart for the Left Front. This 32-row stitch repeat will form pattern throughout.

Shape armhole

Row 87: (RS) Cast off 2 sts, work in pattern to end.

Row 88: (WS) Work in pattern to end.

Row 89: (RS) k3, sl 1, k1, psso, work in pattern to end of row.

Rows 90-99: Repeat rows 89-99 five times until 41 (44, 47) sts on needle.

Rows 100-127: Work in pattern.

Large size: Work two more rows in pattern (129 rows), add two to row total from this point.

Shape neck

Row 128: (WS) Cast off 7 sts, work in pattern to end of row. (34 (37, 40) sts on needle).

Row 129: (RS) Work in pattern to end.

Row 130: (WS) Cast off 1 st, pattern to end.

Rows 131-144: Repeat rows 129-130 seven times until 26 (20, 32) sts on needle.

Rows 145-152: Work in pattern.

Shape shoulder
Row 153: (RS) Cast off 6 (7, 8) sts, pattern to end.
Row 154: Pattern to end.
Rows 155-158: Repeat rows 153-154 twice.
Row 159: Cast off.

Right front
Work as for left front but work stitch repeat from
Right Front chart and reverse all shaping to
alternate sides.

RIGHT FRONT

LEFT FRONT

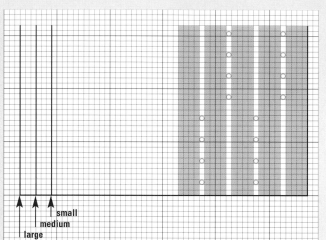

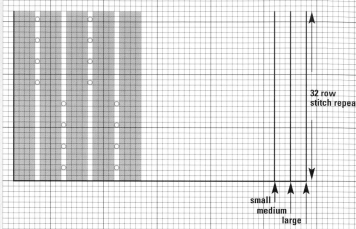

small
medium
large

32 row
stitch repeat

small
medium
large

BACK

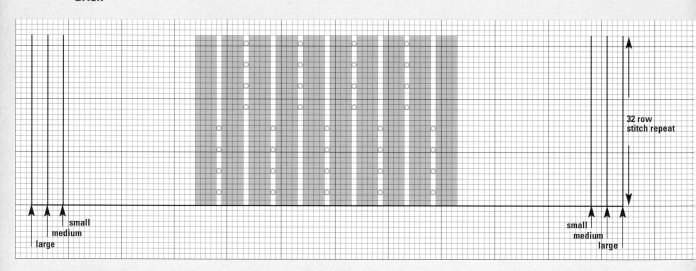

small
medium
large

32 row
stitch repeat

small
medium
large

SLEEVE

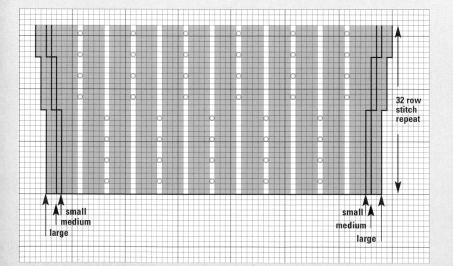

small
medium
large

32 row
stitch
repeat

small
medium
large

Key to charts:

☐ k on RS, p on WS

▨ p on RS, k on WS

○ Make bobble (k1, p1, k1, p1, k1 into next stitch, turn and k5, turn and k5tog)

Back

Cast on 99 (105, 111) sts using 3.75 mm
   (size 5) needles.
Work 16 rows in k1, p1, rib.
Change to 4 mm (size 6) needles and work body
   as follows:
Rows 1-86: Start to work in stitch pattern following
   the chart for the Back. This 32-row stitch repeat
   will form pattern throughout.

Shape armhole

Rows 87-88: Cast off 2 sts, pattern to end.
Row 89: k3, sl 1, k1, psso, work in pattern to last 5
   sts, k2tog, k3.
Row 90: Pattern to end.
Rows 91-100: Repeat rows 89-90 five times until
   83 (89, 95) sts on needle.
Rows 101-152: Work in pattern.
Large size: Work two more rows in pattern (154
   rows), add two to row total from this point.

Shape neck and shoulder

Row 153: (RS) Cast off 6 (7, 8) sts, pattern 17 (19,
   21) sts, k2tog, k3. Place remaining sts on a holder,
   turn to work right side of neck.
Row 154: (WS) Work to end.
Row 155: (RS) Cast off 6 (7, 8) sts, pattern to last
   5 sts, k2tog, k3.
Row 156: Work to end.
Row 157: Cast off 6 (7, 8) sts, pattern to end.
Row 158: Pattern to end.
Row 159: Cast off.

To work left side of neck

Row 153: Rejoin yarn and cast off 27 sts. Then work
   in pattern to end of row and work as for right side
   reversing all shaping.

Sleeves - knit two

Cast on 57 (59, 63) sts using 3.75 mm
   (size 5) needles.
Work 16 rows in k1, p1, rib.
Change to 4 mm (size 6) needles and work sleeve
   as follows:
Rows 1-16: Follow Sleeve chart for stitch pattern.

Shape sleeve

Row 17: (RS) Increase 1 st each side as follows: k3 sts, then knit into front and back of next st, work in pattern to last 5 sts then knit into front and back of next st, k4.

Rows 18-32: Continue in pattern, increasing (as row 17) on row 27.

After the 32 rows, work in stocking stitch throughout.

Rows 33-117: Increase 1 st at each side (as row 17) on row 37 and every following 10th row until 77 (79, 83) sts on needle.

Rows 118-132: Work without shaping.

Shape sleeve head

Rows 133-134: Cast off 4 (4, 5) sts, work to end.

Row 135: (RS) Dec 2 sts each side by, k3, sl 1, k2tog, psso, work to last 6 sts, k3tog, k3.

Row 136: Work to end.

Rows 137-138: Repeat rows 135-136.

Row 139: Dec 1 st each side by, k3, sl 1, k1, psso, work to last 5 sts, k2tog, k3.

Row 140: Work to end.

Rows 141-170: Repeat rows 139-140 fifteen times until 29 (31, 33) sts on needle.

Row 171: Cast off.

Making up

Block and steam all pieces carefully.

Using mattress stitch, join the left and right fronts to back at shoulders and attach sleeves to body, easing the sleeves into armhole. Leave side seams and underarm seams open.

Button band

Cast on 10 sts using 3.75 mm (size 5) needles.

Work in k1, p1, rib for approx 140 rows or until band fits front cardigan edge when gently stretched.

Break yarn, place sts on holder.

Button marking

Mark position for 6 buttons, the first 12 rows from bottom edge, and the last 4 rows from top edge where neck shaping begins. Place the remaining buttons evenly spaced between the first and last.

Buttonhole band

Work as for button band but do not break yarn. Work buttonholes to match marked button positions on button band. Make buttonholes as follows:

Row 1: (RS) Rib 3, cast off 1 st, rib to end.

Row 2: (WS) Rib to last 3 sts, yo, rib to end.

Gently stretch the front bands to fit the front sections so as to achieve a clean edge and stitch into place.

Collar

Using 3.75 mm (size 5) needles, rib across the 10 sts from the right front band then pick up 6 sts across front neck, then 25 sts up front neck edge. Pick up evenly 35 sts around back neck and then pick up 25 sts down front neck, 6 sts across front neck and rib across the 10 sts from right front band (117 sts on needle).

Work in k1, p1, rib for 26 rows. Cast off in stitch repeat.

Join the side seams and underarm seams using mattress stitch.

Sew on buttons.

PROJECT 11:
Chenille Cardigan

This cardigan is both feminine and practical. The chenille yarn is wonderfully tactile, and the looped stitch and rib details on the collar and cuffs give it added textural interest.

Materials
Yarn A: 5 (5, 6) x 100 g balls Rowan Chunky Cotton Chenille, Shade 382/Chunky 100% cotton chenille, red (approx 140 m (153 yd) per 100 g (3½ oz) ball)

Yarn B: 1 (1, 1) x 50 g ball Jaeger Matchmaker Merino Aran, Shade 756/Aran wool, mulberry (approx 82 m (90 yd) per 50 g (1¾ oz) ball)

Needles: 5 mm (size 8), 4.5 mm (size 7) and 4 mm (size 6)

Other: 5 buttons

Check your tension
18 sts x 24 rows to 10 x 10 cm (4 x 4 in) measured over stocking stitch using 4.5 mm (size 6) needles.

Abbreviations
See page 16.

Sizes

	Small	Medium	Large
To fit bust cm (in)	86 (34)	91 (36)	97 (38)
Actual size	91 (36)	97 (38)	102 (40)
Back length	59 (23½)	59 (23½)	59 (23½)
Sleeve underarm	48 (19)	48 (19)	48 (19)

Special abbreviations
ML – make loop: k1, keeping stitch on left hand needle, bring yarn forward, pass yarn over left thumb to make loop, take yarn back and knit this stitch again, slip stitch off needle, then pass first stitch over the loop stitch.

Left front
Cast on 36 (40, 44) sts using 4 mm (size 6) needles and yarn B.

Work hem as follows.

Row 1: (WS) Work in k2, p2 rib to end of row.

Rows 2-5: Change to yarn A. Work in rib.

Rows 6-7: Change to yarn B. Work in rib.

Row 8: Change to yarn A. *k1, ML, repeat from * to last 2 sts, k2.

Row 9: Work in rib as before.

Row 10: k2, *ML, k1, repeat from * to end.

Row 11: Work in rib as before.

Rows 12-13: Change to yarn B. Work in rib as before.

Change to 4.5 mm (size 7) needles. Work in yarn A only.

Row 14: (RS) k2, p2, k2, p2, knit to end.

Row 15: Purl to last 8 sts, k2, p2, k2, p2.

Rows 16-85: Repeat rows 14 and 15.

Shape armhole
Row 86: (RS) Cast off 2 sts, pattern to end.

Row 87: Pattern.

Rows 88: Cast off 1 st, pattern to end.

Rows 89-92: Repeat rows 87-88 twice.

Row 93: Pattern.

Row 94: (RS) Cast off 1 st, knit to end
(30 (34, 38) sts on needle).
Row 95: (WS) Purl.
Rows 96-114: Work in stocking st.
Large size only: Work 2 more rows and add 2 to row
total from this point.

Shape neck
Row 115: (WS) Cast off 3 sts, purl to end.
Row 116: Pattern.
Row 117: Cast off 1 st, purl to end.

Rows 118-129: Repeat rows 116-117 six times until
20, (24, 28) sts on needle.
Rows 130-135: Work in stocking st.

Shape shoulder
Rows 136-142: Cast off 4 (5, 6) sts at beginning of
row 136 and every RS row until 4 sts on needle.
Row 143: Purl.
Rows 144: Cast off.

Right front

Work hem as for left front, except:

Row 8: (RS) Change to yarn A, k2 *ML, k1, repeat from * to end.

Row 10: (RS) *k1, ML, repeat from * to last 2 sts, k2.

Work main body as for left front except:

Row 14: (RS) Knit to last 8 sts, p2, k2, p2, k2.

Row 15: (WS) p2, k2, p2, k2, purl to end.

These 2 rows set stitch pattern. Then work as for left front reversing all shaping and patterning.

Back

Cast on 82 (90, 98) sts using 4 mm (size 6) needles and yarn B.

Work hem as follows:

Row 1: (WS) Work in k2, p2 rib to end of row.

Rows 2-5: (RS) Change to yarn A. Work in rib.

Rows 6-7: Change to yarn B. Work in rib.

Row 8: Change to yarn A. *k1, ML, repeat from * to last 2 sts, k2.

Row 9: Work in rib as before.

Row 10: k2, *ML, k1, repeat from * to end.

Row 11: Work in rib as before.

Rows 12-13: Change to yarn B. Work in rib as before.

Change to 4.5 mm (size 7) needles. Work in yarn A only.

Row 14: (RS) k2, p2, k2, p2, knit to last 8 sts, p2, k2, p2, k2.

Row 15: p2, k2, p2, k2, purl to last 8 sts, k2, p2, k2, p2.

Rows 16-85: Repeat rows 14 and 15.

Shape armhole

Rows 86-87: Cast off 2 sts, pattern to end.

Rows 88-93: Cast off 1 st, pattern to end.

Row 94: (RS) Cast off 1 st, knit to end.

Row 95: Cast off 1 st, purl to end (70 (78, 86) sts on needle).

Rows 96-135: Work in stocking st.

Large size only: Work 2 more rows and add 2 to row total from this point.

Shape shoulder and neck

Row 136: (RS) Cast off 4 (5, 6) sts at beginning of row, k20 (23, 26), place remaining sts on holder, turn to work right side of neck.

Row 137: Cast off 1 st, work to end.

Row 138: Cast off 4 (5, 6) sts, work to end.

Rows 139-143: As rows 137-138 until 4 sts on needle.

Row 144: Cast off.

Rejoin yarn and cast off 22 sts, work to end.

Row 137: (WS) Cast off 4 (5, 6) sts at beginning of row, work to end.

Row 138: Cast off 1 st at beginning of row, work to end.

Rows 139-144: Repeat rows 137-138 twice until 4 sts on needle.

Row 145: Cast off.

Sleeves - knit two

Cast on 42 (44, 46) sts using 4 mm (size 6) needles.

Work hem as follows:

Size: small

Row 1: (WS) Work in k2, p2 rib to last 2 sts, k2.

Rows 2-5: Change to yarn A. Work in rib.

Rows 6-7: Change to yarn B. Work in rib.

Row 8: Change to yarn A. *k1, ML, repeat from * to last 2 sts, k2.

Row 9: Work in rib as before.

Row 10: k2, *ML, k1, repeat from * to end.

Row 11: Work in rib as before.

Rows 12-13: Change to yarn B. Work in rib as before.

Size: medium

Row 1: (WS) Work in k2, p2 rib to end of row.

Rows 2-5: Change to yarn A. Work in rib.

Rows 6-7: Change to yarn B. Work in rib.

Row 8: Change to yarn A. k2, *ML, k1, repeat from * to end of row.

Row 9: Work in rib as before.

Row 10: *k1, ML, repeat from * to last 2 sts, k2.

Row 11: Work in rib as before.

Rows 12-13: Change to yarn B. Work in rib as before.

Size: large

Row 1: (WS) p2, work in k2, p2 rib to end of row.

Rows 2-5: Change to yarn A. Work in rib.

Rows 6-7: Change to yarn B. Work in rib.

Row 8: Change to yarn A. *k1, ML repeat from * to last 2 sts, k2.

Row 9: Work in rib as before.

Row 10: k2, *ML, k1, repeat from * to end.

Row 11: Work in rib as before.

Rows 12-13: Change to yarn B. Work in rib as before.

All sizes

Change to 4.5 mm (size 7) needles.

Rows 14-104: Work in stocking st using yarn A only, increasing on rows 20 and every following 12th row to 58 (60, 62) sts. (Increase 1 st each side by working into the front and back of 2nd st and last st.)

Rows 105-115: Work without shaping

Shape sleeve head

Rows 116-117: Cast off 3 (4, 4) sts, work to end.

Rows 118-147: Cast off 1 st, work to end until 30 (32, 32) sts on needle.

Medium and large sizes: Work 2 more rows until 30 (30) sts on needle.

All sizes: Cast off.

Making up

Block and steam all pieces carefully.

Using mattress stitch, join the left and right fronts to back at shoulders and attach sleeves to body, easing the sleeves into armhole. Leave side seams and underarm seams open.

Button band

Cast on 10 sts using 4 mm (size 6) needles.

Work in hem pattern as for left front.

Row 1: (WS) Work in k2, p2 rib to end of row.

Rows 2-5: Change to yarn A. Work in rib.

Rows 6-7: Change to yarn B. Work in rib.

Row 8: Change to yarn A. *k1, ML, repeat from * to last 2 sts, k2.

Row 9: Work in rib as before.

Row 10: k2, *ML, k1, repeat from * to end.

Row 11: Work in rib as before.

Rows 12-13: Change to yarn B. Work in rib as before.

Work rows 2-13 until band fits front cardigan edge to neck shaping when gently stretched. Cast off.

Button marking

Mark position for 5 buttons, the first 14 rows from bottom edge, and the last 4 rows from top edge where neck shaping begins. Place the remaining buttons evenly spaced between the first and last.

Buttonhole band

Work stitch pattern as for left button band except:

Row 8: (RS) Change to yarn A. k2, *ML, k1, repeat from * to end.

Row 10: (RS) *k1, ML, repeat from * to last 2 sts, k2.

At the same time work buttonholes to match marked button positions on button band, as follows:

Row 1: (RS) Rib 4, cast off 1 st, rib to end.

Row 2: (WS) Rib to last 4 sts, yo, rib to end.

Collar

Cast on 68 sts using 5 mm (size 8) needles and 1 strand of yarn A and yarn B together. Work as follows:

Row 1: (WS) k to end.

Row 2: *k1, ML, repeat from * to last 2 sts, k2.

Row 3: k to end.

Row 4: k2, *ML, k1, repeat from * to end.

Rows 5-16: Repeat rows 1-4 three times.

Then work in stocking st for 2 rows. Cast off.

Attach button bands to the left and right fronts and sew on buttons.

Place centre back of collar to centre of back neck and collar edges to middle of button bands, then stitch into place.

Join the body side and sleeve seams using mattress stitch.

PROJECT 12:
Casual Cable Sweater

This sweater uses a combination of the cable techniques and rib placements to create a dramatic textural statement. It has a great slouchy feel, ideal for the weekends or the outdoors.

Materials
Yarn: 9 (9, 10) x 100 g hanks Rowan Magpie Aran, Shade 320/Aran wool, grey/brown (approx 140 m (153 yd) per 100 g (3½ oz) hank)
Needles: 5 mm (size 8) and 4.5 mm (size 7)

Check your tension
18 sts x 23 rows to 10 x 10 cm (4 x 4 in) measured over stocking stitch using 5 mm (size 8) needles.

Abbreviations
See page 16.

Front
Cast on 108 (116) sts using 4.5 mm (size 7) needles.
Work 10 rows following the hem stitch pattern on Front chart.
Change to 5 mm (size 8) needles and work in pattern following the chart for Front.
Rows 1-100: Repeat these 36 rows throughout.

Sizes

	Small/Medium	Medium/Large
To fit bust cm (in)	86-91 (34-36)	91-97 (36-38)
Actual size	104 (41)	117 (46)
Back length	68 (27)	68 (27)
Sleeve underarm	47 (18½)	47 (18½)

Shape armhole
Rows 101-102: Cast off 3 sts, pattern to end.
Row 103: (RS) Dec 1 st each side as follows: k3, sl 1, k1, psso, work in pattern to last 5 sts, k2tog, k3.
Row 104: Pattern to end.
Rows 105-106: Repeat rows 103-104 (98 (106) sts on needle).
Rows 107-126: Work in pattern.
Medium/large size: Work two more rows (128 rows) and add two to row total from this point.

Shape neck
Row 127: (RS) Pattern for 39 (43) sts, then place remaining sts on holder. Turn to work left side of neck.
Row 128: (WS) Cast off 1 st, pattern to end.
Row 129: (RS) Pattern to end.
Rows 130-131: Repeat rows 128-129 five times until 33 (37) sts on needle.
Rows 140-152: Work without shaping.

Shape shoulder
Row 153: RS facing. Cast off 10 (12) sts, pattern to end.
Row 154: Pattern to end.
Rows 155-156: Repeat rows 153-154 until 13 (13) sts on needle.
Row 157: Cast off.

Work right side of neck
Row 127: (RS) Rejoin yarn and cast off 20 sts, then work as for left side reversing all shaping.

Back

Cast on 108 (116) sts and work as for front until
  the armhole decreasing has been completed.
  (Row 106 – 98 (106) sts on needle.)
Rows 107-150: Work without shaping.
Medium/large size: Work two more rows
  (152 rows) and add two to the row total
  form this point.

Shape back neck and shoulder

Row 151: (RS) k37 (41) sts, place remaining
  sts on holder. Turn to work right side of
  back neck.
Row 152: (WS) Bind off 2 sts, work in
  pattern to end.
Row 153: (RS) Bind off 10 (12) sts, work
  in pattern to end.
Rows 154-155: Repeat rows 152-153
  (13 (13) sts on needle).
Row 156: Work to end.
Row 157: Bind off.

To work left side

Row 151: (RS) Rejoin yarn, bind off 22 sts, work in
  pattern to end.
Then work as for right side reversing all shaping.

Sleeves – knit two

Cast on 62 (66) sts using 4.5 mm (size 7) needles.
Work 10 rows following the hem pattern on the
  Sleeve chart.
Change to 5 mm (size 8) needles.
Work following 36-row stitch repeat from Sleeve
  chart throughout. At the same time shape
  as follows.

Shape sleeve

Rows 1-6: Work without shaping.
Row 7: (RS) k3, inc 1, work to last 5 sts, inc 1, k4.
Rows 8-73: Repeat this inc row every 6 rows until
  86 (90) sts on needle.
Rows 74-100: Work without shaping.

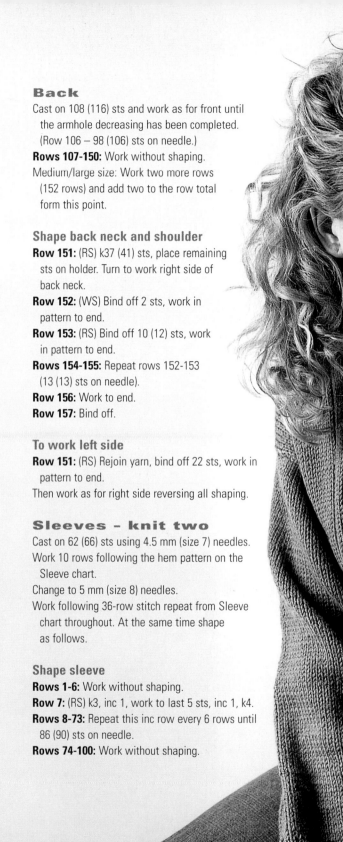

FRONT AND BACK

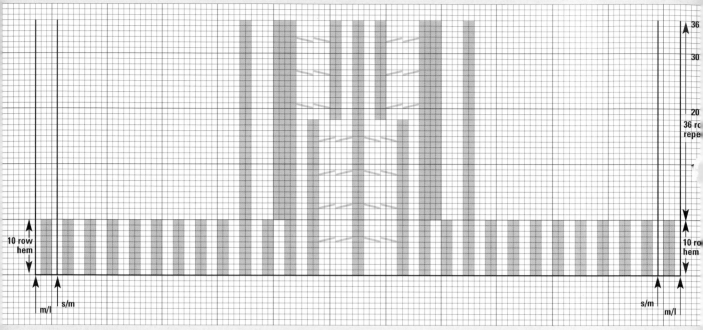

SLEEVES

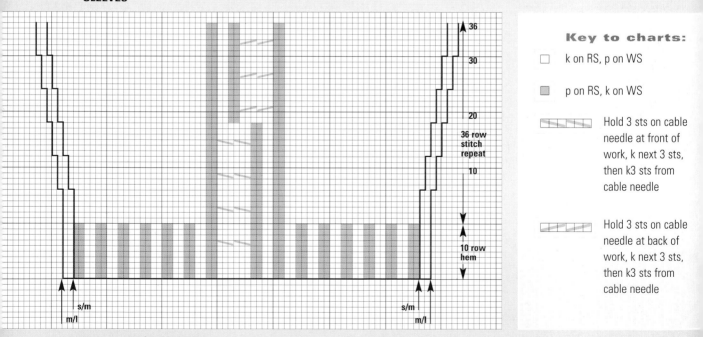

Key to charts:

☐ k on RS, p on WS

▨ p on RS, k on WS

Hold 3 sts on cable needle at front of work, k next 3 sts, then k3 sts from cable needle

Hold 3 sts on cable needle at back of work, k next 3 sts, then k3 sts from cable needle

COLLAR (STITCH REPEAT)

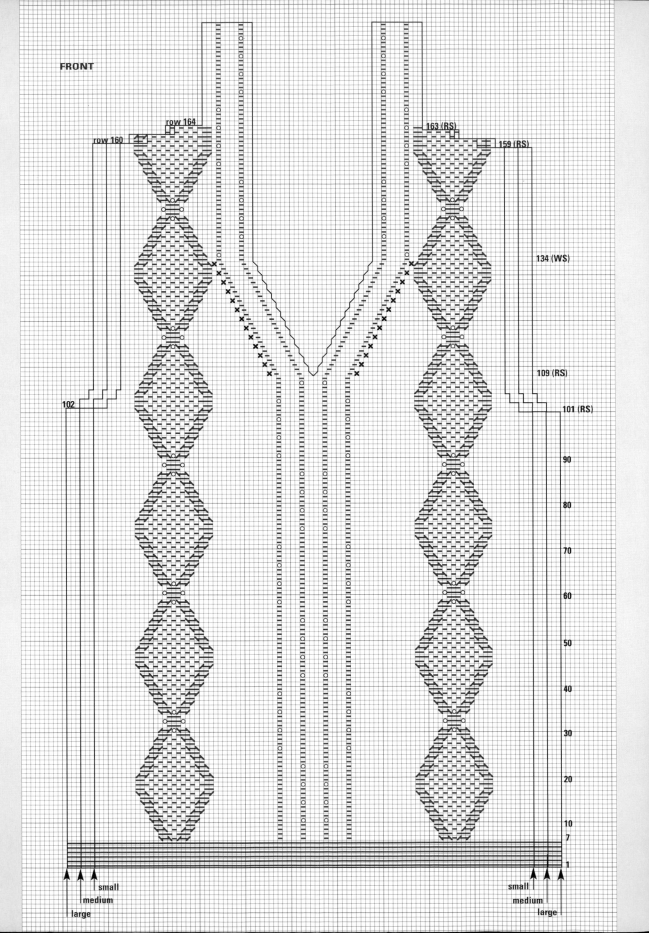

FRONT

row 164

row 160

163 (RS)

159 (RS)

134 (WS)

109 (RS)

102

101 (RS)

90

80

70

60

50

40

30

20

10
7

1

small
medium
large

small
medium
large

BACK

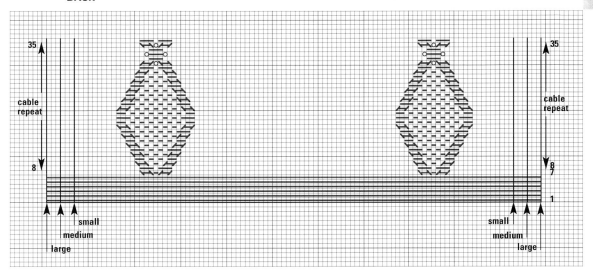

SLEEVE

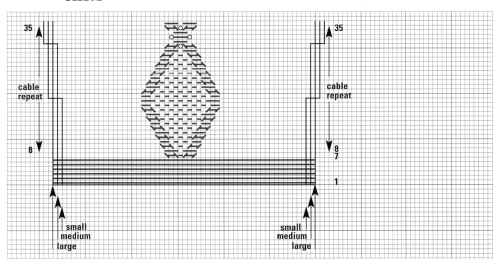

Key to charts:

☐ p on RS, k on WS

➖ k on RS, p on WS

○ Make bobble (k1, p1, k1, p1, k1 into next st, turn, k5, turn, then k5 tog)

✖ p2tog (purl 2 stitches together to shape neck)

◥◣ T3F (twist 3 forward), slip next 2 sts on to cable needle and hold at front of work, purl next st, knit 2 sts from cable needle

◢◤ T3B (twist 3 back), slip next st on to cable needle and hold at back of work, knit next 2 sts, purl st held on cable needle

Right side of neck

Row 109: (RS) Rejoin yarn and work in pattern for 8 sts, p2tog, pattern to end of row. Repeat this every RS row until 29 (32, 35) sts remain. Continue to work as for left side reversing all shaping.

Back

Cast on 96 (102, 108) sts using 4 mm (size 6) needles.
Rows 1-6: Stocking stitch.
Rows 7-100: Change to 4.5 mm (size 7) needles and work in pattern following the chart for Back.

Shape armhole

Rows 101-102: Cast off 3 sts, pattern to end.
Rows 103-104: Cast off 2 sts, pattern to end.
Rows 105-106: Cast off 1 st, pattern to end.
Rows 107-156: Pattern.

Shape back neck and shoulder

Row 157: (RS) Pattern 22 (25, 28) sts, place remaining sts on holder. Turn to work right side of back neck.
Row 158: Pattern.
Row 159: Cast off 6 (7, 8) sts, pattern to end.
Row 160: Cast off 2 sts, pattern to end.
Rows 161-162: As rows 159-160.
Row 163: Cast off.

Left side

Row 157: (RS) Rejoin yarn and cast off 40 sts, pattern to end.
Then work as for right side, reversing all shaping.

Sleeves – knit two

Cast on 53 (55, 57) sts using 4 mm (size 6) needles and work as follows:
Rows 1-6: Stocking stitch.
Row 7: (RS) Change to 4.5mm (size 7) needles and work in pattern following the chart for Sleeve.
Rows 8-19: Pattern.

Shape sleeve

Row 20: (WS) k2, inc 1, work to last 3 sts, inc 1, k2.
Rows 21-104: Pattern, repeating inc row every 12 rows (69 (71, 73) sts on needle).
Rows 105-120: Pattern.

Shape sleeve head

Rows 121-122: Cast off 3 (3, 4) sts, pattern to end.
Rows 123-124: Cast off 2 sts, pattern to end.
Rows 125-126: Cast off 1 st, pattern to end.
Rows 127-148: Repeat rows 125-126 until 35 (37, 37) sts on needle. Cast off.

Making up

Block and steam all pieces carefully.
Using mattress stitch, join the front to back at shoulders.
Join the neck band strips at centre back and attach to back neck of sweater.
Join the sleeves to body, easing the sleeve head into the armhole.
Join the side seams and underarm seams, WS facing together so that the seams are on the outside, and stitch 3 sts in from edge so that the seams curl back as a feature.

Neck band

Using a 4 mm (size 6) circular needle, pick up 24 sts down front left neck, 14 sts across left front neck shaping, 14 sts up right front neck shaping, 24 sts up front right neck and 30 sts across the back neck. Work in stocking stitch for 6 rows, then cast off.

ANTIQUE KNITS

Lacy, decorative stitches and surfaces are combined with mercerised yarn to inspire a feeling of the 1930s. Feminine silhouettes are combined with lace patterns, decorative edges and beading to create a sophisticated, glamorous feel.

PROJECT 14:
Decorative-edge Top

This design uses the beading technique and introduces the idea of decorative edges. The top also has a decorative edged rib hem which gives it a hip-hugging 30s feel.

Materials
Yarn: 7 (7, 8) x 50 g balls Jaeger Aqua Cotton, Shade 329/100% cotton DK, maroon (approx 106 m, 115 yd per 50 g (1¾ oz) ball)
Needles: 4 mm (size 6) and 3.25 mm (size 3)
Other: Approx 400 beads

Check your tension
22 sts x 30 rows to 10 x 10 cm (4 x 4in) measured over stocking stitch using 4 mm (size 6) needles.

Abbreviations
See page 16.

Special abbreviations
KB1 – knit into back of next stitch.
mb – move bead, hold yarn at front of work, slip a stitch purlwise, place bead, then move yarn to back of work.

Note: Before you start knitting, thread approx 55 beads on each ball of yarn.

Sizes

	Small	Medium	Large
To fit bust cm (in)	86 (34)	91 (36)	97 (38)
Actual size	91 (36)	97 (38)	102 (40)
Back length	57 (22½)	57 (22½)	57 (22½)
Sleeve length	5 (2)	5 (2)	5 (2)

Front
Cast on 150 (159, 168) sts using 3.25 mm (size 3) needles.
Row 1: (WS) *Cast off 2 sts, k1 (already on RH needle), repeat from * to end of row (50 (53, 56) sts on needle).
Row 2: (RS) *k1, yf, repeat from * to last st, k1 (99 (105, 111) sts on needle).
Row 3: *k1, KB1, repeat from * to last st, k1.
Row 4: *k1, p1, repeat from * to last st, k1.
Row 5: *p1, k1, repeat from * to last st, p1.
Rows 6-27: k1, p1, rib as set.
Change to 4 mm (size 6) needles and stocking stitch.
Rows 28-33: Work in stocking st.
Row 34: (RS) k4 (7, 1), *mb, k8, repeat from * to last 5 (8, 2) sts, mb, k4 (7, 1).
Row 35: Purl.
Row 36: Knit.
Row 37: Purl.
Row 38: Knit.
Row 39: Purl.
Row 40: Knit.
Row 41: Purl.
Rows 34-41 form the pattern repeat. Work in pattern throughout.
Rows 42-107: Work in pattern.

Shape armhole
Rows 108-109: Cast off 2 sts, pattern to end.
Rows 110-121: Cast off 1 st, pattern to end until 83 (89, 95) sts on needle.
Rows 122-175: Work in pattern.

Shape neck

Row 176: (RS) Work 22 (25, 28) sts in pattern, then place remaining sts on holder, turn to work left side of neck.

Row 177: Cast off 2 sts, pattern to end.

Row 178: Pattern.

Rows 179-182: Repeat rows 177-178 twice until 16 (19, 22) sts on needle.

Row 183: Pattern.

Shape shoulder

Row 184: (RS) Cast off 5 (6, 7) sts, pattern to end.

Row 185: Pattern.

Rows 186-187: Repeat rows 184-185 until 6 (7, 8) sts on needle.

Row 188: Cast off.

To work right side of neck

Row 176: Rejoin yarn and cast off 39 sts. Work in pattern to end.

Row 177: Pattern.

Row 178: (RS) Cast off 2 sts, pattern to end.

Rows 179-182: Repeat rows 177-178 twice until 16 (19, 22) sts on needle.

Rows 183-184: Pattern.

Shape shoulder

Row 185: (WS) Cast off 5 (6, 7) sts, pattern to end.

Row 186: Pattern.

Rows 187-188: Repeat rows 185-186 until 6 (7, 8) sts on needle.

Row 189: Cast off.

Back

Work as for front until row 121 is completed.

Rows 122-181: Work in pattern.

Shape neck and shoulder

Row 182: (RS) Pattern 20 (23, 26) sts, then place remaining sts on holder, turn to work right side of neck.

Row 183: Cast off 2 sts, pattern to end.

Row 184: Cast off 5 (6, 7) sts, pattern to end.

Rows 185-186: Repeat rows 183-184.

Row 187: Pattern.

Row 188: Cast off.

To work left side of neck

Rejoin yarn and cast off 43 sts, then work to end of row. Then work as for right side reversing all neck and shoulder shaping.

Sleeves – knit two

Cast on 72 (74, 76) sts using 3.25 mm (size 3) needles.

Change to 4 mm (size 6) needles and work 2 rows in stocking st, then work in bead pattern as for front and back; row 3 sets the start of pattern.

Row 3: (RS) k4 (5, 6), *mb, k8, repeat from * to last 5 (6, 7) sts, mb, k4 (5, 6).

Work in pattern throughout, and at the same time shape sleeve head as follows:

Shape sleeve head

Rows 5-6: Cast off 2 sts, pattern to end.

Rows 7-36: Cast off 1 st, pattern to end until 38 (40, 42) sts on needle.

Rows 37-38: Pattern.

Row 39: Cast off.

Sleeve edging

Work lengthways. Cast on 7 sts using 3.25 mm (size 3) needles.

Note: Sts should only be counted after the 4th row.

Row 1: (RS) k1, k2tog, (yf) twice, k2tog, (yf) twice, k2.

Row 2: k3, *p1, k2, repeat from *.

Row 3: k1, k2tog, (yf) twice, k2tog, k4.

Row 4: Cast off 2 sts, k4, p1, k2.

These 4 rows form repeat. Continue in pattern until edge measures width of sleeve hem cast on edge.

Stitch edging to hem of sleeve neatly.

Making up

Block and steam all pieces carefully.
Using mattress stitch, join the right front shoulder
to back.

Neck band

Use 3.25 mm (size 3) needles. Pick up 11 sts down
the left front neck, then pick up 39 sts along the
front neck edge, 11 sts up right front neck, and 52
sts around back neck (113 sts on needle). Work
4 rows in 1x1 rib, then cast off in rib.

Join left shoulder seam and neck trim.
Attach sleeves to body, easing the
sleeve head into the armhole. Join
the side and sleeve seams using
mattress stitch.

PROJECT 15:
Beaded Cardigan

This simple cardigan uses the beading technique explained in the Basic Skills section of the book. It uses a crisp, glazed yarn and, depending on how you style it, can be worn for evening or day wear. This cardigan looks particularly good when teamed with antique buttons.

Materials
Yarn: 10 (10, 11) x 50 g balls Rowan Cotton Glace, Shade 806/100% cotton, maroon (approx 115 m (125 yd) per 50 g (1¾ oz) ball)
Needles: 3.25 mm (size 3) and 2.75 mm (size 2)
Other: Approx 2,000 small beads; 6 buttons

Check your tension
23 sts x 32 rows to 10 x 10 cm (4 x 4 in) measured over stocking stitch using 3.25 mm (size 3) needles.

Abbreviations
See page 16.

Note: Before you start knitting, thread approximately 200 beads on each ball of yarn.

Left front
Cast on 52 (57, 62) sts using 2.75 mm (size 2) needles.
Work 4 rows in moss st.
Change to 3.25 mm (size 3) needles.
Rows 5-112: Work in pattern from Left Front chart. Rows 9-14 form pattern repeat. Work in pattern throughout.

Shape armhole
Row 113: (RS) Cast off 2 sts, pattern to end.
Row 114: Pattern.
Row 115: Cast off 1 st, pattern to end.
Rows 116-125: Repeat rows 114-115 five times until 44 (49, 54) sts on needle.
Rows 126-139: Work in pattern.

Shape neck
Row 140: (WS) Cast off 12 sts, pattern to end.
Row 141: Pattern.
Row 142: Cast off 1 st, pattern to end.
Rows 143-158: Repeat rows 141-142 eight times until 23 (28, 33) sts on needle.
Rows 159-178: Pattern without shaping.

Shape shoulder
Row 179: (RS) Cast off 5 (6, 7) sts, pattern to end.
Row 180: Pattern
Rows 181-184: Repeat rows 179-180 twice until 8 (10, 12) sts on needle.
Row 185: Cast off.

Sizes

	Small	Medium	Large
To fit bust cm (in)	86 (34)	91 (36)	97 (38)
Actual size	91 (36)	97 (38)	102 (40)
Back length	55 (22)	55 (22)	55 (22)
Sleeve underarm	47 (18½)	47 (18½)	47 (18½)

Right front

Cast on 52 (57, 62) sts using 2.75 mm (size 2) needles.

Work 4 rows in moss st.

Change to 3.25 mm (size 3) needles.

Rows 5-113: Work in pattern from Right Front chart, making buttonholes on row 41 and every following 20th row, ie, rows 61, 81, etc.

Rows 9-14 form pattern repeat. Work in pattern throughout.

Make buttonholes: Moss 2, yo, k2tog, pattern to end.

Shape armhole

Row 114: (WS) Cast off 2 sts, pattern to end.

Row 115: Pattern.

Row 116: Cast off 1 st, pattern to end.

Rows 117-126: Repeat rows 115-116 five times until 44 (49, 54) sts on needle.

Row 127-140: Work in pattern.

Shape neck

Row 141: (RS) Cast off 12 sts, pattern to end.

Row 142: Pattern.

Row 143: Cast off 1 st, pattern to end.

Rows 144-159: Repeat rows 142-143 eight times until 23 (28, 33) sts on needle.

Rows 160-179: Work in pattern.

Shape shoulder

Row 180: (WS) Cast off 5 (6, 7) sts, pattern to end.

Row 181: Pattern.

Rows 182-185: Repeat rows 180-181 twice until 8 (10, 12) sts on needle.

Row 186: Cast off.

Back

Cast on 103 (113, 123) sts using 2.75 mm (size 2) needles.

Work 4 rows in moss st.

Change to 3.25 mm (size 3) needles.

Rows 5-112: Work in pattern from Back chart.

Rows 9-14 form pattern repeat. Work in pattern throughout.

LEFT FRONT

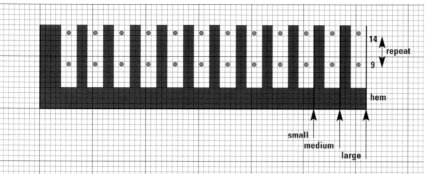

14
repeat
9
hem

small
medium
large

RIGHT FRONT

14
repeat
9
hem

small
medium
large

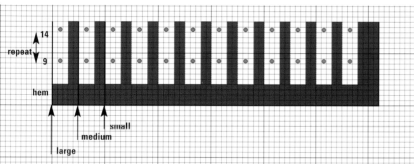

Key to charts:

☐ k on RS, p on WS

■ Work in moss stitch (k1, p1)

● Place bead (yarn forward, slide
bead and hold at front of work,
slip next stitch purlwise, keep
yarn at front, yarn back)

BACK

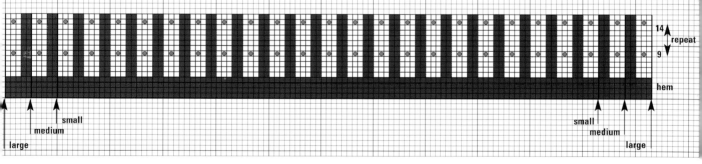

14
repeat
9
hem

small
medium
large

small
medium
large

SLEEVES

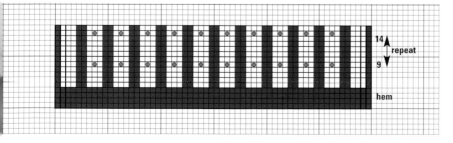

14
repeat
9
hem

Shape armhole
Rows 113-114: Cast off 2 sts, pattern to end.
Rows 115-126: Cast off 1 st, pattern to end until 87 (97, 107) sts on needle.
Rows 127-178: Work in pattern.

Shape back neck and shoulder
Row 179: (RS) Cast off 5 (6, 7) sts, pattern 21 (25, 29) sts, place remaining sts on a holder, then turn to work right side of neck.
Row 180: (WS) Cast off 1 st, pattern to end.
Rows 181-184: Repeat rows 179-180 twice until 8 (10, 12) sts on needle.
Row 185: Cast off.

To work left side
(RS) Rejoin yarn and cast off 35 sts, then work in pattern to end.
Row 180: Cast off 5 (6, 7) sts at beginning of row, then work in pattern to end.
Row 181: Cast off 1 st at beginning of row, work in pattern to end.
Rows 182-185: As rows 180 and 181 twice until 8 (10, 12) sts on needle.
Row 186: Cast off.

Sleeves - knit two
Cast on 56 (58, 60) sts using 2.75 mm (size 2) needles.
Work 4 rows in moss st as for back and fronts.
Change to 3.25 mm (size 3) needles.
Rows 5-18: Work in pattern from Sleeve chart.
Rows 9-14 form pattern repeat. Work in pattern throughout.

Shape sleeve
Row 19: (RS) Increase 1 st each side by working into the front and back of 2nd st and last st.
Rows 20-127: Repeat this increase row every 12 rows until 76 (78, 80) sts on needle.
Rows 128-152: Work without shaping.

Shape sleeve head
Row 153-154: Cast off 2 (3, 4) sts, pattern to end.
Rows 155-184: Cast off 1 st, pattern to end until 42 sts on needle.
Row 185: Cast off.

Assembly
Block and steam all pieces carefully.
Using mattress stitch, join the fronts to back at shoulders.

Neck band
Use 2.75 mm (size 2) needles. Pick up 12 sts from the right front neck, then pick up 15 sts from the right front neck shaping, 20 sts up front neck, 44 sts around back neck and then 20 sts down left front neck, 15 sts down front shaping and then 12 sts across left front neck (138 sts on needle).
Row 1: Work in moss st.
Row 2: Make buttonhole: moss 2, yo, k2tog, moss to end. Work 2 more rows in moss st. Cast off.

Attach sleeves to body, easing the sleeve head into the armhole. Join the side and sleeve seams using mattress stitch. Sew on buttons.

PROJECT 16:
Lacy Drawstring Bag

This project is a lovely accessory piece and makes an ideal gift for someone. It combines an easy lace technique, a decorative edge and a beaded drawstring detail to make a simple yet luxurious statement.

Materials
Yarn: 1 x 50 g ball each Rowan Cotton Glace, Shades 787 and 806/100% cotton, mauve and maroon (approx 115 m (125 yd) per 50 g (1¾ oz) ball (if one colour, only 1 x 50 g (1¾ oz) ball required))
Needles: 3.25 mm (size 3) single-pointed and 2.75 mm (size 2) double-pointed
Other: Approx 80 beads

Check your tension
26 sts x 36 rows to 10 x 10 cm (4 x 4 in) measured over stitch pattern using 3.25 mm (size 3) needles.

Abbreviations
See page 16.

Special abbreviations
M1 – make 1 stitch. Pick up horizontal strand of yarn lying between stitch just worked and next stitch, and knit it.

Bag
Cast on 39 sts using 3.25 mm (size 3) needles and using contrast colour. Work in pattern as follows:
Note: sts should only be counted after the 2nd and 4th row of this pattern.
Row 1: (RS) k1, *k2tog, repeat from * to end.
Row 2: k1, *M1, k1, repeat from * to end.
Row 3: *k2tog, repeat from * to last st, k1.
Row 4: Repeat row 2.
Rows 5-12: Repeat rows 1-4, twice.

Change to main colour.
Rows 13-108: Repeat rows 1-4, twenty-four times.
Change to contrast colour.
Rows 109-120: Repeat rows 1-12.
Row 121: Cast off.

Edging
Work lengthways.
Cast on 10 sts using 3.25 mm (size 3) needles and contrast colour.
Note: sts should only be counted after the 8th row.
Row 1: (RS) k3, *yf, k2tog, repeat from * (yf) twice, k2tog, k1.
Row 2: k3, p1, k2, *yf, k2tog, repeat from *, k1.
Row 3: k3, *yf, k2tog, repeat from *, k1, (yf) twice, k2tog, k1.
Row 4: k3, p1, k3,*yf, k2tog, repeat from *, k1.
Row 5: k3, *yf, k2tog, repeat from *, k2, (yf) twice, k2tog, k1.
Row 6: k3, p1, k4, *yf, k2tog, repeat from *, k1.
Row 7: k3, *yf, k2tog, repeat from *, k6.
Row 8: Cast off 3 sts, k5, *yf, k2tog, repeat from *, k1.
These 8 rows form stitch pattern.
Rows 9-80: Repeat rows 1-8 nine times.
Row 81: Cast off.

Beaded drawstring

Thread beads on to main colour yarn.

Cast on 2 sts using 2.75 mm (size 2)
  double-pointed needles.

Row 1: k2. Do not turn work. Bring yarn from end of
  row on left side and draw tightly across back of
  work to the beginning of row, k2.

Rows 2-4: Repeat row 1.

Row 5: k1, place bead, p1.

Repeat these five rows until drawstring is
  approximately 140 cm (55 in).

Cast off.

Making up

Fold cast-off edge to cast-on edge of bag and
  sew side seams, using mattress stitch.

Attach decorative edging to top edge of bag
  and stitch/graft in place. Thread drawstring
  through edging.

PROJECT 17:
Lace Cardigan

This cardigan uses a faggotted rib pattern to create the illusion of a combination of lace, rib and slip stitch textures. The decadent feel is enhanced by a glazed yarn and beaded buttons.

Materials
Yarn: 10 (10, 11) x 50 g balls Jaeger Aqua 100% cotton DK, Shade 306/DK cotton, grey (approx 106 m (115 yd) per 50 g (1¾ oz) ball)
Needles: 4 mm (size 6) and 3.75 mm (size 5)
Other: 10 buttons

Check your tension
22 sts x 30 rows to 10 x 10 cm (4 x 4 in) measured over stocking stitch using 4 mm (size 6) needles.

Abbreviations
See page 16.

Left front
Cast on 50 (55, 60) sts using 3.75 mm (size 5) needles.
Change to 4 mm (size 6) needles.
Work in pattern throughout as follows.
Row 1: (RS) k1, * k2tog, yf, k1, yf, sl 1, k1, psso, rep from * to last 9 sts, k1, k5, yf, k2tog, k1.
Row 2: (WS) Purl.
Rows 1-2 form pattern repeat.
Rows 3-90: Work in pattern.

Shape armhole
Row 91: (RS) Cast off 3 sts, work to end.
Row 92: (WS) Purl to end.
Row 93: (RS) Cast off 1 st, work to end.
Row 94: Purl to end.
Rows 95-102: Repeat rows 93-94 four times until 42 (47, 52) sts on needle.
Rows 103-121: Work without shaping.

Shape neck
Row 122: (WS) Cast off 10 sts, purl to end.
Row 123: (RS) Pattern to end.
Row 124: Cast off 2 sts, purl to end.
Row 125: Pattern to end.
Row 126: Cast off 1 st, purl to end.
Rows 127-136: Repeat rows 125-126 five times until 24 (29, 34) sts on needle.
Rows 137-146: Work in pattern without shaping.

Shape shoulder
Row 147: (RS) Cast off 8 sts, pattern to end.
Row 148: Purl to end.
Rows 149-150: Repeat rows 147-148 (8 (13, 18) sts on needle).
Row 151: Cast off.

Sizes
	Small	Medium	Large
To fit bust cm (in)	86 (34)	91 (36)	97 (38)
Actual size	91 (36)	97 (38)	102 (40)
Back length	55 (22)	55 (22)	55 (22)
Sleeve underarm	47 (18½)	47 (18½)	47 (18½)

Right front

Cast on 50 (55, 60) sts using 3.75 mm
  (size 5) needles.
Change to 4 mm (size 6) needles.
Work in pattern throughout as follows.
Row 1: (RS) k1, k2tog, yf, k5, k1, * k2tog, yf,
  k1, yf, sl 1, k1, psso, rep from * to last st, k1.
Row 2: (WS) Purl.
Rows 1-2 form pattern repeat.
Rows 3-91: Work in pattern.

Shape armhole

Row 92: (WS) Cast off 3 sts, purl to end.
Row 93: (RS) Pattern to end.
Row 94: (WS) Cast off 1 st, purl to end.
Rows 95-102: Repeat rows 93-94 four times until
  42 (47, 52) sts on needle.
Rows 103-120: Work without shaping in pattern.

Shape neck

Row 121: (RS) Cast off 10 sts, pattern to end.
Row 122: (WS) Purl to end.
Row 123: Cast off 2 sts, pattern to end.
Row 124: Purl to end.
Row 125: Cast off 1 st, pattern to end.
Rows 126-135: Repeat rows 124-125 five times
  until 24 (29, 34) sts on needle.
Rows 136-145: Work without shaping.

Shape shoulder

Row 146: (WS) Cast off 8 sts, purl to end.
Row 147: Pattern to end.
Rows 148-149: Repeat rows 146-147 (8 (13, 18) sts
  on needle).
Row 150: Cast off.

Back

Cast on 97 (107, 117) sts using 3.75 mm
  (size 5) needles.
Change to 4 mm (size 6) needles.
Work in pattern throughout as follows.
Row 1: (RS) k1, * k2tog, yf, k1, yf, sl 1, k1, psso,
  rep from * to last st, k1.
Row 2: (WS) Purl.
These 2 rows form pattern repeat.
Rows 3-90: Work in pattern.

Shape armhole

Rows 91-92: RS facing. Cast off 2 sts, pattern
  to end.
Rows 93-100: Cast off 1 st, pattern to end until
  85 (95, 105) sts on needle.
Rows 101-146: Work without shaping in pattern.

Shape neck and shoulder

Row 147: (RS) Cast off 8 sts, pattern 18 (23, 28) sts,
  then place remaining sts on a holder, turn to work
  right side of neck.
Row 148: (WS) Cast off 2 sts, purl to end of row.
Row 149: (RS) Cast off 8 sts, pattern to end
  (8 (13, 18) sts on needle).
Row 150: (WS) Purl to end.
Row 151: Cast off.

To work left side of neck

Row 147: Rejoin yarn and cast off 33 sts. Then work
  in pattern to end of row and work as for
  right side reversing all shaping.

Sleeves - knit two

Cast on 47 sts using 3.75 mm (size 5) needles.
Change to 4 mm (size 6) needles.
Work in pattern as follows.
Row 1: (RS) k1, * k2tog, yf, k1, yf, sl 1, k1, psso,
  repeat from * to last st, k1.
Row 2: (WS) Purl.
Rows 1-2 form pattern repeat.
Rows 3-13: Work in pattern.
Shape sleeve as follows (try to remain in pattern):
Row 14: (WS) Increase 1 st each side as follows.
  p1, purl into front and back of next st, purl to last
  2 sts, purl into front and back of next st, p1.
Rows 15-102: Repeat this increase row every 8
  rows until 71 sts on needle.
Rows 103-122: Work without shaping.

Shape sleeve head

Rows 123-124: Cast off 3 sts, pattern to end.
Rows 125-128: Cast off 2 sts, pattern to end.
Rows 129-152: Cast off 1 st, pattern to end until
  33 sts on needle.
Row 153: Cast off.

Making up

Block and steam all pieces carefully.
Using mattress stitch, join the left and right fronts
  to back at shoulders and attach sleeves to body,
  easing the sleeves into armhole. Leave side seams
  and underarm seams open.

Neck band

Using 3.75 mm (size 5) needles, pick up 10 sts
  across right front neck, 24 sts up right front neck,
  36 sts across back neck, 23 sts down left front
  neck and 10 sts across left front neck.
Row 1: (WS) Knit.
Row 2: (RS) Knit.
Repeat these 2 rows once more,
  then cast off.

Mark position for 10 buttons,
  the first button 5 cm
  (2 in) from the bottom
  edge and the last in
  neck band. Then
  evenly space the
  remaining buttons
  between the first and the
  last. Use the eyelet details
  on the cardigan edge as the
  buttonholes. Sew on buttons.

Join the side seams of back and front
  body leaving 5 cm (2 in) vent at lower
  edge (see photograph). Join underarm
  sleeve seams.

Index

Yarn suppliers

Rowan yarns

Rowan yarns are available from all good department stores. For further information call Rowan Yarns direct on: 01484 681 881 or visit their website: www.knitrowan.com

For information on suppliers outside the U.K., contact the Rowan distributor in your country:

Australia
Australian Country Spinners
314 Albert Street
Brunswick
Victoria 3056
Tel: (03) 9380 3888

Canada
Diamond Yarn
9697 St Laurent
Montreal
Quebec H3L 2N1
Tel: (514) 388 6188

Diamond Yarn
155 Martin Ross, Unit 3
Toronto
Ontario M3J 2L9
Tel: (416) 736 6111
Email: diamond@diamondyarn.com
www.diamondyarns.com

New Zealand
Alterknitives
PO Box 47961
Auckland
Tel: (64) 9 376 0337

Knitworld
Shop 210b, Cuba Mall
Wellington
Tel: (64) 4 385 1918

U.S.A.
Rowan USA
4 Townsend West, Suite 8
Nashua
New Hampshire 03063
Tel: (603) 886 5041/5043
Email: wfibers@aol.com